Smart Meetings, Better Results

Actionable Steps to Lead Engaging and Productive Discussions

Smart Meetings, Better Results- Actionable Steps to Lead Engaging and Productive Discussions

Copyright © 2024 by Angel Marqués
All rights reserved.

No part of this book may be reproduced, stored in a retrieval system, or transmitted in any form or by any means—electronic, mechanical, photocopying, recording, or otherwise—without prior written permission from the author, except in the case of brief quotations for book reviews or similar purposes permitted by copyright law.

This is a work of non-fiction. All content and interpretations herein are based on research and analysis by the author. Any resemblance to real persons, living or dead, is purely coincidental.

Published by Angel Marqués Sánchez
ISBN: 9798303143203

Hello! I would greatly appreciate it if you could share your opinion by leaving a review on Amazon. Reviews not only help other readers discover the book, but they're also essential for supporting future projects.

If you have a few minutes, please visit the review page by scanning the QR code below.

Contents

Chapter 1: Why Meetings Matter 5

Chapter 2: Meeting Types and Objectives 11

Chapter 3: The Role of Preparation 25

Chapter 4: The Art of Facilitation 38

Chapter 5: Building Engagement and Collaboration 52

Chapter 6: Problem-Solving and Decision-Making 68

Chapter 7: Leveraging Technology in Meetings 79

Chapter 8: Ensuring Accountability and Follow-Up 93

Chapter 9: Measuring Meeting Effectiveness 105

Chapter 10: Cultivating a Meeting Culture 118

Chapter 1: Why Meetings Matter

Meetings are a cornerstone of professional life, serving as vital touchpoints for collaboration, communication, and decision-making. In a world driven by teamwork and interconnected goals, meetings act as the bridge between individuals, teams, and departments, ensuring that everyone moves in the same direction. They are not just a routine fixture of the workplace; they are moments where ideas converge, strategies align, and problems are solved.

When done well, meetings become powerful drivers of progress. A well-planned meeting can inspire creativity, resolve conflicts, and clarify complex issues that require collective input. They provide opportunities for individuals to share their insights and for teams to develop solutions that are greater than the sum of their parts. Effective meetings can lead to innovations, strengthen bonds among colleagues, and build trust within organizations. They act as the glue holding projects together and the launching pad for initiatives that bring long-term success.

However, the true value of meetings goes beyond just achieving objectives. They create a shared sense of purpose and urgency, helping to establish a rhythm for work processes. When scheduled and structured thoughtfully, meetings allow organizations to communicate priorities, establish accountability, and foster an environment where every voice matters. They ensure that no one is working in a vacuum, reinforcing the idea that collaboration is the key to sustained achievement.

Despite their potential, meetings often carry a mixed reputation. For some, they are indispensable tools for progress; for others, they represent wasted time and unproductive discussion. This chapter begins by exploring both sides of the equation, laying the foundation for a deeper understanding of how meetings can transform from dreaded obligations into opportunities for meaningful impact.

THE ROLE OF MEETINGS IN PROFESSIONAL SETTINGS

Meetings play a crucial role in the fabric of professional settings, acting as structured opportunities for individuals and teams to exchange information, align on objectives, and make critical decisions. They are the mechanisms by which organizations maintain cohesion, ensuring that goals and strategies are understood across diverse roles and responsibilities. In many ways, meetings serve as the heartbeat of workplace communication, offering spaces where clarity replaces confusion, and collective focus drives outcomes.

The primary function of meetings is to facilitate communication, providing a forum for ideas to be shared and feedback to be exchanged. This is particularly important in organizations where teams operate across different disciplines or geographical locations. Meetings create a shared understanding, bridging gaps that might otherwise hinder collaboration. Whether it is a project kickoff, a brainstorming session, or a performance review, the essence of a meeting lies in bringing people together to achieve something that cannot be accomplished individually.

Beyond communication, meetings are instrumental in fostering collaboration. They provide a platform for pooling expertise, resolving conflicts, and generating solutions that benefit from diverse perspectives. Teams use meetings to synchronize their efforts, allocate resources, and plan the next steps in a way that ensures alignment and minimizes duplication of work. The collaborative nature of meetings empowers individuals to feel heard and valued, strengthening team morale and reinforcing a culture of mutual respect.

Meetings also play a strategic role in decision-making processes. They enable managers and stakeholders to analyze data, weigh options, and commit to courses of action with the confidence that multiple viewpoints have been considered. This collective approach to decision-making often results in stronger outcomes, as it leverages the knowledge and experience of the group rather than relying on a single perspective. Moreover, meetings ensure transparency in decisions, fostering trust and accountability within the organization.

In addition to their direct outcomes, meetings serve an often-overlooked but essential function: reinforcing organizational culture. They are opportunities to model behaviors such as active listening, open dialogue, and respect for differing opinions. Effective meetings demonstrate a commitment to inclusivity and collaboration, showing employees that their contributions are both needed and appreciated. Over time, this strengthens engagement and loyalty, making meetings not just a procedural necessity but a cornerstone of a thriving workplace.

Despite the undeniable value meetings bring when conducted well, their importance is often obscured by poor execution. For meetings to fulfill their role in professional settings, they must be purposeful, inclusive, and results-oriented. Understanding these dynamics lays the groundwork for exploring how meetings can be transformed from routine encounters into powerful tools for achieving professional success.

The Problem with Poorly Run Meetings

Poorly run meetings are a pervasive challenge in professional settings, often leading to frustration, wasted time, and diminished productivity. Despite their intention to bring people together for progress, these meetings frequently fall short, becoming a drain on resources and morale. The consequences ripple through organizations, affecting not just the immediate participants but also the broader workflows and goals they are meant to support.

One of the most common issues with ineffective meetings is the lack of a clear purpose or agenda. Without a defined objective, meetings tend to drift aimlessly, consuming time without delivering value. Participants may leave such gatherings unclear about what was decided or why they were even present. The absence of structure leads to discussions that are either overly broad or frustratingly narrow, making it difficult to achieve meaningful outcomes.

Another prevalent problem is poor time management. Meetings that run too long, veer off-topic, or start and end inconsistently disrupt schedules and reduce the time available for focused work. Conversely, meetings that are too short or rushed fail to cover necessary ground, leaving participants feeling unprepared or unsatisfied. Both scenarios create inefficiencies that undermine the intended purpose of the meeting.

Participant engagement is another critical factor in meeting success, and poorly run meetings often fail in this regard. Monotonous presentations, one-sided discussions, or environments where certain voices dominate can alienate attendees, leading to disengagement and apathy. This lack of engagement not only diminishes the quality of input during the meeting but also hampers buy-in for decisions made, as disengaged participants are less likely to feel invested in the outcomes.

The composition of the meeting itself can also be problematic. Inviting too many participants dilutes the focus, as discussions become unwieldy and harder to manage. Conversely, excluding key stakeholders or relevant contributors leads to gaps in decision-making and the need for follow-up conversations, further prolonging the process. In both cases, the effectiveness of the meeting is compromised.

Poor follow-up is another hallmark of ineffective meetings. Even if the discussion is productive, failing to document decisions, assign action items, or communicate next steps renders the effort meaningless. Participants may leave with differing interpretations of what was agreed upon, resulting in confusion and stalled progress. Over time, this lack of follow-through erodes trust in the value of meetings altogether.

The cumulative effect of poorly run meetings is significant. Studies consistently show the high cost of wasted time in meetings, both financially and in terms of lost productivity. Beyond these tangible losses, there is an emotional toll as well—employees feel frustration, resentment, and even burnout when they perceive their time is not respected. This can lead to disengagement not just from meetings, but from their roles within the organization.

Recognizing these common pitfalls is the first step toward addressing them. Poorly run meetings are not an inevitability; they are the result of inadequate planning, execution, and follow-up. By understanding the factors that contribute to their ineffectiveness, individuals and organizations can begin to implement strategies to transform meetings into productive, empowering experiences that support their goals.

THE VISION OF A WELL-CONDUCTED MEETING

A well-conducted meeting is more than just a scheduled gathering; it is a focused, dynamic, and purposeful event that drives meaningful outcomes. It is a space where ideas are exchanged, decisions are made, and alignment is achieved, leaving participants with a clear sense of progress and direction. The vision of such a meeting is grounded in intentionality, efficiency, and inclusivity, ensuring that every moment spent contributes to the broader goals of the team and organization.

At the heart of a successful meeting is clarity of purpose. Before the meeting even begins, its objectives are well-defined and communicated to participants. Whether the goal is to brainstorm new ideas, solve a specific problem, or review project progress, everyone involved understands the purpose and the desired outcomes. This clarity ensures that the meeting stays focused, with discussions and actions aligned to achieve its aims.

An essential feature of a well-run meeting is effective preparation. The agenda is thoughtfully crafted, outlining key topics, time allocations, and the roles of each participant. Relevant materials are distributed in advance, allowing attendees to arrive prepared and informed. This groundwork sets the stage for meaningful contributions, reducing time spent on unnecessary explanations and enabling a deeper focus on the issues at hand.

Engagement and collaboration define the atmosphere of an effective meeting. All participants are encouraged to contribute, fostering a sense of inclusion and shared ownership of the outcomes. The meeting leader skillfully guides the discussion, ensuring that every voice is heard while keeping the conversation productive and on track. Constructive dialogue flourishes, with differing perspectives viewed as opportunities for growth rather than obstacles.

A hallmark of a great meeting is its efficiency. Time is used wisely, with discussions kept relevant and distractions minimized. The meeting begins and ends on schedule, respecting participants' commitments and reinforcing the value of their time. Decisions are made with confidence, supported by well-facilitated discussions that ensure clarity and consensus.

Inclusivity is another key element of a well-conducted meeting. The right people are in the room—those whose input is essential to achieving the meeting's objectives. Their roles are clear, and their contributions are valued. Conversely, those whose presence is not directly relevant are not burdened with attending, ensuring that every participant feels their time is being used meaningfully.

The impact of an effective meeting extends beyond its conclusion. Action items and decisions are clearly documented, and responsibilities are assigned. Follow-up communication ensures accountability, with participants understanding their next steps and deadlines. This seamless transition from discussion to action reinforces the purpose of the meeting and ensures its outcomes are realized.

A well-conducted meeting also inspires and energizes. Participants leave with a sense of accomplishment, motivated by the progress made and their role in it. They feel connected to the larger goals of the team and organization, and their confidence in the value of meetings is strengthened. This positive experience not only boosts individual morale but also fosters a culture where meetings are seen as opportunities for collaboration and innovation.

The vision of a well-run meeting is not an unattainable ideal; it is the result of intentional practices and a commitment to excellence. By prioritizing preparation, engagement, efficiency, and follow-through, meetings can become powerful tools for driving success and building stronger teams. In the chapters ahead, we will explore the strategies and techniques that can transform this vision into a consistent reality for organizations of all sizes and industries.

Chapter 2: Meeting Types and Objectives

Understanding meeting types is essential because it serves as the foundation for running effective, results-driven discussions. Meetings are not just moments where individuals come together to talk; they are strategic tools that can significantly influence organizational success. However, when meetings lack clarity in purpose or structure, they often lead to wasted time, disengagement, and frustration. Differentiating meeting types ensures that each gathering has a specific focus and aligns with its intended purpose, whether it's brainstorming ideas, making decisions, or sharing updates. By recognizing these distinctions, organizations can transform meetings into powerful drivers of collaboration and productivity rather than dreaded interruptions.

One of the most common issues in workplaces is the blending of multiple meeting purposes into a single session, which inevitably dilutes effectiveness. For example, a brainstorming meeting that inadvertently veers into decision-making can stifle creativity as participants may feel pressured to converge on solutions prematurely. Similarly, progress update meetings that attempt to tackle problem-solving can derail schedules and leave team members unclear about priorities. These scenarios illustrate how a lack of understanding about meeting types can lead to confusion, frustration, and ultimately, a failure to achieve desired outcomes. Identifying and separating meeting types allows leaders and participants to better allocate their focus and energy.

Moreover, understanding meeting types is crucial because it fosters accountability and alignment. Each meeting should contribute to a broader organizational goal, and when its type is clearly defined, participants can easily grasp their role and expectations. For instance, in a decision-making meeting, stakeholders know they are there to analyze data and commit to a course of action. In contrast, a brainstorming session encourages open dialogue and creativity without immediate pressure to finalize solutions. This clarity not only improves individual engagement but also ensures that meetings align with strategic objectives, reducing the risk of miscommunication or wasted effort.

Clear meeting types also enable better preparation, which is vital for productive discussions. When participants know the meeting's purpose and type, they can prepare relevant materials, data, or ideas to contribute effectively. A well-defined meeting agenda tailored to its type sets the stage for efficient discussions and minimizes the chances of veering off course. For instance, a status update meeting benefits from structured progress reports, while a problem-solving meeting might require participants to analyze specific challenges beforehand. This targeted preparation saves time and maximizes the value derived from the session.

Differentiating meeting types cultivates a culture of respect and engagement within teams. When meetings have clear objectives and structures, participants feel that their time is valued and their input is meaningful. This respect fosters a sense of purpose, making employees more likely to engage actively and contribute thoughtfully. Over time, organizations that prioritize understanding meeting types build a reputation for running effective and efficient discussions, boosting morale and enhancing overall productivity. Thus, appreciating the importance of meeting types is not just about improving individual sessions; it's a step toward creating a high-performance culture where collaboration thrives.

DIFFERENTIATING BETWEEN MEETING TYPES

Differentiating between meeting types is a critical step in ensuring that every discussion serves its intended purpose and delivers value. Meetings come in various forms, each designed to achieve a specific goal, and understanding these distinctions is essential for effective planning and execution. By categorizing meetings based on their objectives, participants can better align their expectations, contributions, and energy to the task at hand. This clarity not only improves the quality of discussions but also reduces the inefficiencies caused by overlapping or unclear meeting agendas. Recognizing the unique characteristics of each meeting type is key to ensuring their success.

One common type is the **brainstorming meeting**, which prioritizes creativity and the generation of new ideas. These meetings are typically informal, encourage open-ended discussion, and thrive on the diversity of perspectives. The goal is not to reach a decision but to explore possibilities and think outside the box. Tools such as whiteboards, sticky notes, or digital brainstorming platforms often play a central role in facilitating idea generation. Participants are encouraged to suspend judgment and focus on quantity over quality, creating a pool of ideas that can later be refined. Misusing this meeting type—such as pressuring participants to choose solutions on the spot—can undermine its purpose and limit creative outcomes.

In contrast, **decision-making meetings** are structured and outcome-focused. Their primary goal is to analyze options, weigh pros and cons, and agree on a specific course of action. These meetings often involve fewer participants, typically stakeholders or leaders with the authority to make final decisions. Unlike brainstorming sessions, decision-making meetings require a high level of preparation, including data analysis, pre-meeting discussions, and clarity about decision criteria. A lack of structure in this type of meeting can lead to delays or disagreements, so facilitators must guide the discussion toward actionable resolutions. Successful decision-making meetings conclude with a clear plan and assigned responsibilities.

Another distinct type is the **progress or status update meeting**, which is designed to inform participants about ongoing work, align efforts, and identify any roadblocks. These meetings are usually recurring and relatively brief, with each participant providing a concise update on their area of responsibility. The focus is on sharing information rather than engaging in lengthy discussions or problem-solving. To ensure efficiency, it's crucial to set strict time limits and avoid diving too deeply into issues that require separate meetings. Without discipline, status updates can become drawn-out and unproductive, defeating their purpose of keeping the team synchronized.

Problem-solving meetings, on the other hand, are dedicated to addressing specific challenges and developing actionable solutions. These meetings require a focused agenda and often benefit from structured frameworks such as root cause analysis, the "5 Whys" technique, or SWOT (Strengths,

Weaknesses, Opportunities, Threats) analysis. The participants typically include individuals with relevant expertise or a stake in the outcome. A well-facilitated problem-solving meeting avoids blame-shifting and focuses on collaboration to identify effective resolutions. If the meeting's purpose is not clearly defined, it risks devolving into unproductive debate or frustration.

Specialized meetings such as **one-on-one discussions** or **all-hands meetings** serve unique roles within organizations. One-on-ones are personal and private, often used for performance reviews, feedback, or mentoring. They foster trust and alignment between managers and team members. All-hands meetings, by contrast, are large-scale sessions aimed at company-wide communication, often led by senior leadership to share updates, celebrate achievements, or reinforce organizational values. Both types require different approaches to preparation and execution, highlighting the importance of tailoring meeting structures to their intended audience and purpose.

Differentiating between meeting types ensures that discussions remain focused, productive, and goal-oriented. By aligning each meeting's format with its specific purpose, leaders and participants can better manage their time and resources. Understanding these distinctions also minimizes the risk of misaligned expectations, enabling every meeting to contribute meaningfully to organizational objectives. When meetings are clearly defined and well-structured, they become effective tools for collaboration, decision-making, and innovation.

ALIGNING MEETING TYPES TO BUSINESS GOALS

Aligning meeting types to business goals is essential for ensuring that every meeting contributes to organizational success. Meetings are not standalone events; they are tools to advance broader objectives, whether it's driving innovation, improving operational efficiency, or fostering team cohesion. Misaligned meetings—those that lack a connection to business priorities—waste time, dilute focus, and often leave participants unclear about their purpose. When meeting types are deliberately chosen and strategically aligned with specific goals, they become valuable opportunities to steer the organization toward desired outcomes.

The first step in aligning meeting types to business goals is to clearly define the purpose of the meeting in relation to the organization's objectives. For instance, if the goal is to launch a new product, the meetings leading up to the launch might include brainstorming sessions to generate ideas, decision-making meetings to finalize strategies, and progress updates to monitor timelines. Each meeting type should serve as a building block toward achieving the larger goal. Without this clarity, meetings can become fragmented, leading to redundant conversations or irrelevant discussions that hinder progress rather than advancing it.

Choosing the right meeting type also ensures that participants' roles and contributions are aligned with organizational priorities. For example, a decision-making meeting about a budget reallocation should involve key stakeholders who understand the financial implications and strategic priorities of the organization. In contrast, a brainstorming meeting for marketing campaign ideas might benefit from the creative input of cross-functional team members. Aligning the type and purpose of the meeting with the specific participants ensures that the right voices are heard, promoting efficiency and relevance. This alignment also prevents the inclusion of unnecessary attendees, reducing disruptions and fostering more focused discussions.

A critical aspect of this alignment is preparing a clear agenda that connects the meeting's purpose to actionable outcomes. An agenda should specify not only what will be discussed but also how the meeting's results will impact the organization's broader goals. For example, a progress update meeting might include agenda items like "review milestones against Q1 objectives" and "identify risks to achieving targets." Similarly, a problem-solving meeting could focus on resolving a specific operational challenge tied to the company's performance metrics. By explicitly linking agenda items to business priorities, the meeting gains a sense of purpose that motivates participants and drives accountability.

Another important consideration is evaluating the frequency and necessity of meetings to ensure they align with ongoing business needs. Over-scheduling meetings can drain resources and pull employees away from other strategic work. For example, recurring status updates should only be held if they directly contribute to aligning teams with evolving goals or identifying risks early. Leaders must assess whether a meeting is genuinely needed or if its purpose could be achieved through alternative methods, such as email updates or collaborative tools. When meetings are carefully calibrated to support business objectives, they become an asset rather than a drain on time and productivity.

Aligning meeting types to business goals fosters a results-driven culture where meetings are seen as opportunities to achieve tangible outcomes. When participants see a direct link between a meeting and the organization's strategic vision, they are more likely to engage actively and contribute meaningfully. Over time, this alignment reinforces a mindset where meetings are valued not for their occurrence but for the results they produce. By deliberately matching meeting types to organizational objectives, businesses can create a meeting culture that prioritizes effectiveness, collaboration, and progress, ensuring that every discussion moves the organization closer to its goals.

Identifying Clear and Measurable Objectives

Identifying clear and measurable objectives is critical to ensuring that meetings are productive and purposeful. A well-defined objective acts as a guiding star, giving participants clarity about the meeting's purpose and what success looks like. Without a clear objective, meetings often become unfocused, resulting in wasted time and unproductive discussions. Objectives help ensure that participants are aligned, discussions remain on track, and outcomes are actionable. They also establish accountability, as measurable goals make it easy to determine whether the meeting achieved its intended results.

To identify clear objectives, it's essential to start by asking, **"Why are we meeting?"** This fundamental question helps distinguish between necessary and unnecessary meetings and clarifies the meeting's purpose. For example, a meeting may be called to brainstorm ideas, make a decision, solve a problem, or provide updates. Each purpose requires a different approach and structure, so defining it upfront is key. A brainstorming session might aim to "generate at least 20 creative ideas for a new marketing campaign," while a decision-making meeting could have the goal of "choosing the top vendor from a shortlist of three." These objectives are specific and give participants a clear understanding of what the meeting aims to accomplish.

Objectives should be both **specific** and **measurable** to ensure they are actionable. The SMART framework—Specific, Measurable, Achievable, Relevant, and Time-bound—is a useful tool for defining meeting objectives. For instance, instead of setting a vague goal like "discuss project updates," a SMART objective would be "review the progress of all project milestones against the Q2 timeline and identify two areas requiring immediate attention." Such clarity not only directs the meeting's flow but also ensures that all participants come prepared with relevant information and insights. A specific and measurable objective keeps the meeting grounded in actionable outcomes.

Communicating the meeting objective to participants in advance is equally important. Sending out a meeting invitation with a detailed agenda that includes the objective helps attendees prepare effectively and aligns their expectations. For example, if the objective is to resolve a specific customer issue, participants can bring relevant data or insights to contribute meaningfully to the discussion. Clear communication also prevents misunderstandings about the meeting's purpose, reducing the chances of irrelevant discussions or unnecessary debates. A shared understanding of the objective ensures that everyone is working toward the same outcome from the outset.

Another critical step in setting measurable objectives is to define what success looks like for the meeting. Success metrics can vary depending on the meeting type and purpose. For instance, the success of a decision-making meeting might be judged by whether the group reached a consensus and outlined next steps. In a brainstorming session, success could be measured by the number and quality of ideas generated. For a status update meeting, success might mean ensuring all team members understand the project's current status and are aligned on priorities. By identifying these metrics before the meeting, organizers can assess its effectiveness afterward and refine their approach for future sessions.

Clear and measurable objectives transform meetings from aimless gatherings into focused, results-driven discussions. They establish a framework that keeps participants on task, fosters accountability, and ensures that the time invested in the meeting translates into tangible outcomes. By defining objectives, communicating them effectively, and measuring their achievement, leaders can make meetings more efficient and impactful. Over time, consistently identifying and achieving clear objectives can help create a meeting culture where discussions are purposeful and contribute meaningfully to organizational success.

BRINGING IT ALL TOGETHER

Bringing it all together, effective meetings are the result of a deliberate and thoughtful approach that incorporates understanding meeting types, aligning them with business goals, and defining clear, measurable objectives. Each of these elements plays a critical role in ensuring that meetings are productive, engaging, and impactful. Without a clear structure, meetings risk becoming unproductive distractions, but when planned with purpose and precision, they become valuable tools for driving collaboration, innovation, and organizational success.

The first step to successful meetings is recognizing that not all meetings are the same. By differentiating between meeting types—such as brainstorming, decision-making, status updates, or problem-solving—leaders can ensure that each gathering has a focused purpose. This differentiation not only helps participants understand their roles but also allows the meeting facilitator to tailor the structure and process to the desired outcomes. For example, a brainstorming session thrives on open-ended discussion, while a decision-making meeting requires structure and preparation. Understanding these distinctions is fundamental to planning meetings that work.

Aligning meeting types to business goals ensures that every discussion serves a larger purpose and contributes to the organization's strategic objectives. Meetings that are disconnected from these goals can feel like a drain on time and energy, leaving participants frustrated. However, when meetings are clearly linked to business priorities, they become opportunities to make progress on key initiatives. For example, a team working on a product launch might organize specific meetings to drive innovation, finalize decisions, and track progress—all of which directly support the overarching business objective. This alignment creates a sense of purpose and accountability that motivates participants to engage meaningfully.

Clear and measurable objectives are the cornerstone of effective meetings. A well-defined objective keeps discussions focused, ensuring that participants know exactly why they are there and what they are expected to accomplish. SMART objectives (Specific, Measurable, Achievable, Relevant, and Time-bound) provide a useful framework for setting these goals, whether the meeting is designed to generate ideas, solve problems, or make decisions. For example, an objective like "generate 10 actionable ideas for the next quarter's marketing strategy" gives the meeting a clear endpoint, enabling participants to work toward a shared goal with precision and efficiency.

Preparation and communication are also critical components that bring these principles together. Sharing the meeting's purpose, type, and objectives with participants in advance ensures that everyone arrives informed and ready to contribute. A thoughtfully designed agenda, aligned with the meeting's goals, helps keep discussions on track and prevents unnecessary deviations. Post-meeting follow-ups, such as distributing action items or decisions, reinforce accountability and ensure that outcomes are implemented effectively. Together, these steps create a seamless process that maximizes the value of each meeting.

Successful meetings depend on intentionality and a commitment to continuous improvement. By combining a clear understanding of meeting types, alignment with business goals, and the use of measurable objectives, organizations can create a culture where meetings are respected and valued. This holistic approach not only enhances the productivity and impact of individual meetings but also fosters a collaborative environment where teams feel empowered to solve problems, make decisions, and drive innovation. When all these elements come together, meetings become powerful tools for achieving organizational success.

Bringing everything together, this chapter emphasizes the importance of understanding meeting types, aligning them with business goals, and identifying clear, measurable objectives. These foundational elements ensure meetings are purposeful, productive, and directly tied to achieving organizational success. To help you implement these principles effectively, the following tools and resources are provided as actionable takeaways from the chapter:

Tools and Resources for Effective Meetings

1. Meeting Types Comparison Table

This table provides an overview of different meeting types, their purposes, key participants, and expected outcomes. Use this as a reference when planning your meetings to ensure you select the right type for your goals.

Meeting Type	Purpose	Key Participants	Expected Outcomes
Brainstorming	Generate creative ideas	Cross-functional teams	A list of actionable ideas
Decision-Making	Make final decisions	Stakeholders, leadership	A clearly agreed-upon decision
Progress Updates	Share progress on tasks	Team members, project leads	Alignment on priorities and next steps

Meeting Type	Purpose	Key Participants	Expected Outcomes
Problem-Solving	Resolve specific issues	Relevant stakeholders, SMEs	Practical solutions to identified challenges

How to Use:

Before scheduling a meeting, refer to this table to confirm the type that best aligns with your purpose and participants.

---

2. Framework for Choosing the Right Meeting Type

This step-by-step framework simplifies the process of selecting the appropriate meeting type based on your objectives.

Step 1: Identify the primary purpose of your meeting.

- Is it to generate ideas? → Choose **Brainstorming**.
- Is it to finalize a decision? → Choose **Decision-Making**.
- Is it to share progress updates? → Choose **Status Updates**.
- Is it to address a challenge? → Choose **Problem-Solving**.

Step 2: Define the necessary participants.

- Broad groups for creativity → Brainstorming.
- Decision-makers and stakeholders → Decision-Making.
- Team members or project leads → Status Updates.
- Subject-matter experts for analysis → Problem-Solving.

Step 3: Match the structure to your objective.

- Open-ended discussion for brainstorming.

- Structured debate and consensus-building for decision-making.
- Concise updates with time limits for progress reviews.
- Analytical approaches for problem-solving.

How to Use:

Use this framework to assess the purpose of your meeting before sending out invitations or creating an agenda.

---

3. SMART Objective Template

Defining clear, measurable objectives is essential for a successful meeting. Use this template to draft objectives that are **Specific, Measurable, Achievable, Relevant,** and **Time-bound**:

Template for Meeting Objectives:

- **Specific:** What is the exact purpose of the meeting?
- **Measurable:** How will you know the goal was achieved?
- **Achievable:** Is the goal realistic for this meeting?
- **Relevant:** How does the objective align with organizational priorities?
- **Time-Bound:** When should the goal be completed?

Example Objective:

"By the end of this meeting, finalize the top two project priorities for Q2 (specific and measurable), ensuring they align with quarterly revenue goals (relevant), and assign responsible team leads within 30 minutes (time-bound and achievable)."

How to Use:

Draft an objective for every meeting using this template and share it with participants beforehand to align expectations.

---

4. Pre-Meeting Preparation Checklist

Preparation is the key to running effective and focused meetings. This checklist ensures you're fully prepared before the meeting begins:

- ☑ Define the purpose and type of the meeting.
- ☑ Use the SMART framework to set a clear objective.
- ☑ Prepare a detailed agenda aligned with the objective.
- ☑ Identify and invite only the necessary participants.
- ☑ Share the agenda and any preparatory materials with participants in advance.

How to Use:

Run through this checklist before every meeting to ensure it is well-planned and aligned with its goals.

Final Thoughts and Action Steps

Now that you understand how to differentiate meeting types, align them with business objectives, and define clear objectives, you're equipped to transform how your meetings operate. Use the tools and frameworks provided in this chapter as practical guides to structure and evaluate your meetings. Start by reviewing your next meeting's purpose and applying these steps to ensure it delivers real value. Over time, these practices will not only improve individual meetings but also contribute to a culture of efficiency and purpose-driven collaboration within your organization.

By mastering the principles in this chapter, you take a critical step toward ensuring that every meeting is an opportunity for progress, not just another item on the calendar.

Chapter 3: The Role of Preparation

Preparation is the cornerstone of a successful meeting, setting the stage for clarity, engagement, and actionable results. Without adequate preparation, even the most well-intentioned meetings can devolve into aimless conversations or frustrating exchanges, leaving participants feeling drained and unproductive. A lack of preparation often manifests in wasted time, miscommunication, and unresolved issues that ripple through an organization. On the other hand, a well-prepared meeting builds a foundation for purposeful dialogue, aligning participants and ensuring that every minute spent contributes toward defined objectives. This chapter begins with a focus on understanding why preparation is indispensable in professional settings.

One of the most significant advantages of preparation is the clarity it brings to the meeting's purpose and direction. When the organizer takes the time to outline the goals and structure of a meeting, it removes ambiguity for all participants. Preparation helps define the "why" behind the gathering—whether it's to brainstorm ideas, make decisions, or share critical updates—and ensures that everyone in the room or on the call understands the value of their involvement. This clarity motivates participants to engage fully, knowing that the meeting is relevant to their roles and responsibilities.

Preparation also enables efficient use of time, arguably one of the most valuable resources in any organization. A well-prepared meeting ensures that discussions remain focused and progress steadily toward the intended outcomes. Without preparation, meetings often meander, with participants struggling to agree on priorities or action steps. By investing time in pre-meeting planning, organizers can structure the conversation to avoid such inefficiencies, allocating time for each topic and keeping distractions at bay. This level of forethought demonstrates respect for everyone's schedules, fostering a culture of professionalism and accountability.

Another critical reason preparation matters is the confidence and readiness it instills in both the facilitator and the participants. A facilitator who has prepared thoroughly is better equipped to guide discussions, address concerns, and adapt to unexpected challenges. They enter the meeting with a clear plan, exuding confidence that encourages trust and cooperation among attendees. Similarly, when participants receive the agenda or preparatory materials ahead of time, they can come prepared with insights, questions, or ideas, enriching the quality of the conversation. This shared sense of readiness elevates the overall effectiveness of the meeting.

Preparation also sets the tone for collaboration, creating an environment where participants feel empowered to contribute meaningfully. By defining roles and expectations in advance, the organizer ensures that every attendee knows how they fit into the larger picture. This reduces confusion and prevents scenarios where individuals feel sidelined or uncertain about their role. When attendees are informed and aligned beforehand, it fosters a sense of collective purpose, making it easier to achieve consensus and drive results during the meeting itself.

Preparation is not merely a logistical necessity but a strategic advantage that transforms meetings from mundane routines into opportunities for progress and innovation. It bridges the gap between intention and execution, ensuring that meetings deliver tangible value to the organization and its people. By recognizing the importance of preparation and making it a non-negotiable part of the process, leaders and teams can set the stage for consistently impactful discussions. This commitment to preparation reflects a broader mindset of intentionality and excellence that resonates far beyond the confines of a single meeting.

DEVELOPING AN AGENDA

Developing an agenda is one of the most critical aspects of meeting preparation, serving as the blueprint that guides discussions and ensures the meeting stays on track. An agenda is not just a list of topics; it is a strategic tool that defines the purpose of the meeting, organizes priorities, and sets the tone for the interactions. Without a well-crafted agenda, meetings can drift aimlessly, with participants unsure of what to focus on or how to contribute effectively. A thoughtful agenda establishes structure and clarity, making it a vital element for achieving meaningful outcomes.

The first step in creating an effective agenda is to articulate the meeting's primary objective. This involves identifying what the meeting is meant to accomplish, whether it is to solve a problem, make a decision, brainstorm ideas, or update a team on key developments. Defining this objective ensures that every item on the agenda aligns with the meeting's purpose. A focused agenda helps prevent discussions from veering into unrelated topics, saving time and maintaining the attention of all participants. It also clarifies the expectations for everyone involved, setting the stage for a productive and goal-oriented conversation.

Timing is another essential factor in agenda development. Allocating specific time slots to each topic not only structures the meeting but also creates a sense of urgency and momentum. When participants know there is a limited time for discussion, they are more likely to stay focused and concise in their contributions. Prioritizing topics is equally important, with high-priority items placed earlier in the agenda to ensure they receive adequate attention. This approach safeguards against running out of time for critical discussions and allows for flexibility if less urgent topics need to be postponed or addressed briefly.

A well-crafted agenda also designates roles and responsibilities, ensuring that participants know what is expected of them before and during the meeting. This might include identifying presenters for specific topics, assigning someone to take notes, or designating a facilitator to guide the discussion. These roles help distribute the workload and keep the meeting dynamic, with different individuals leading various segments. When participants are aware of their responsibilities in advance, they come prepared and ready to contribute, elevating the overall quality of the meeting.

Lastly, an agenda is not just a tool for the facilitator; it is a communication tool for the entire group. Sharing the agenda with participants before the meeting allows them to familiarize themselves with the topics and prepare relevant insights or questions. This pre-meeting engagement encourages a sense of ownership among attendees, fostering active participation and collaboration. When participants understand the agenda's structure and goals, they are more likely to align their contributions with the meeting's objectives, resulting in a more cohesive and impactful discussion.

An agenda is far more than a checklist—it is the backbone of an effective meeting, providing clarity, structure, and direction. It reflects the organizer's forethought and respect for participants' time, creating an environment conducive to meaningful dialogue and actionable results. Developing an agenda requires intentionality, but the rewards it brings in terms of focus, engagement, and outcomes are well worth the effort. When done correctly, the agenda transforms a meeting from a mundane obligation into a strategic opportunity for progress. To bring this concept to life, consider a sample agenda template that illustrates how to structure an effective meeting. A well-crafted agenda typically includes the following sections:

1. **Meeting Title and Date:** Clearly label the agenda with the meeting's purpose and when it will take place.

2. **Objective:** Define the primary goal of the meeting in a concise statement, such as "to finalize the marketing strategy for Q1" or "to brainstorm solutions for customer retention challenges."

3. **Topics and Discussion Points:** List each item to be addressed, organized in a logical order. Include bullet points or sub-items to clarify the scope of each topic.

4. **Time Allocations:** Assign specific time slots for each topic to manage the flow and ensure balanced discussions.

5. **Roles and Responsibilities:** Identify who will lead each discussion point, present information, or facilitate decisions, as well as any specific participant roles, such as note-taker or timekeeper.

By using this template as a guide, meeting organizers can create agendas that set clear expectations, keep discussions focused, and maximize productivity. Sharing a template like this also provides consistency across meetings, allowing teams to collaborate more efficiently and build trust in the meeting process.

PRE-MEETING COMMUNICATION AND PARTICIPANT ALIGNMENT

Pre-meeting communication and participant alignment are essential components of successful meeting preparation, acting as the bridge between planning and execution. Effective communication ensures that all participants are informed and aligned with the meeting's goals, roles, and expectations before they even step into the room or join a call. This proactive approach minimizes confusion, fosters readiness, and enhances the quality of participation. When communication is clear, timely, and purposeful, it creates a sense of shared responsibility and collaboration, setting the stage for a focused and productive meeting.

The first element of pre-meeting communication is providing participants with all the relevant information they need to prepare adequately. This includes the meeting agenda, any supporting materials, and details about the logistics, such as the time, location, or virtual platform to be used. Sharing this information well in advance gives attendees the opportunity to review and reflect on the topics at hand, gather necessary resources, and formulate their thoughts or questions. By empowering participants with this context, the meeting becomes less about impromptu reactions and more about thoughtful, informed discussions that drive results.

Participant alignment is equally crucial and involves ensuring that the right people are invited and understand their roles in the meeting. The effectiveness of any meeting largely depends on the composition of its attendees—those who have the knowledge, authority, or skills needed to address the topics on the agenda. Misalignment in participation can lead to wasted time, as individuals who lack the necessary context struggle to contribute meaningfully, or critical stakeholders are missing when decisions need to be made. Communicating the rationale for each person's inclusion and their expected contributions helps them prepare effectively and reinforces the importance of their presence.

Another key aspect of pre-meeting communication is setting clear expectations for engagement and outcomes. Participants should understand not only what the meeting is about but also what is expected from them during the session. This might include reviewing documents, preparing presentations, or coming ready to share specific insights. Clear expectations reduce ambiguity and ensure that everyone arrives prepared to play an active role. Additionally, it creates accountability, as participants recognize their responsibilities in contributing to the meeting's success.

Effective communication also addresses the emotional and psychological readiness of participants. A meeting can sometimes evoke anxiety or resistance, particularly if contentious issues are on the agenda. Pre-meeting communication can help mitigate these concerns by framing the meeting's purpose positively and inclusively. For example, emphasizing the meeting as an opportunity for collaboration and problem-solving rather than as a platform for criticism can shift participants' mindsets. This alignment fosters a sense of trust and openness, making it easier to navigate complex or sensitive topics.

Pre-meeting communication and participant alignment are not merely preparatory steps; they are strategic investments in the success of the meeting. By ensuring that participants are informed, aligned, and engaged before the meeting begins, organizers create a strong foundation for meaningful dialogue and actionable outcomes. Clear, purposeful communication transforms meetings from reactive to proactive, empowering participants to contribute thoughtfully and collaboratively. When this alignment is prioritized, the meeting becomes a more cohesive, efficient, and impactful experience for everyone involved.

ROLE OF COMPANY POLICIES IN MEETING PREPARATION

Company policies play a pivotal role in meeting preparation, providing a framework that promotes consistency, efficiency, and alignment with organizational goals. These policies establish standardized practices for how meetings should be planned, conducted, and followed up on, helping to streamline processes and avoid confusion. By adhering to these guidelines, employees and leaders alike can ensure that meetings serve their intended purposes and contribute to the broader objectives of the organization. In essence, company policies act as a guiding compass for meeting preparation, fostering a culture of intentionality and professionalism.

One of the key benefits of incorporating company policies into meeting preparation is the establishment of clear expectations around structure and format. Policies often dictate the use of standardized templates for agendas, action plans, and follow-up reports, ensuring that all meetings share a common framework. This consistency reduces the cognitive load for participants, as they know what to expect and how to navigate the meeting process. For organizers, these templates serve as a starting point, making the preparation process more efficient and less prone to oversight. Such practices also enhance cross-departmental collaboration by eliminating discrepancies in how meetings are approached.

Timing and frequency are other critical aspects governed by company policies. Policies may specify acceptable durations for different types of meetings, such as limiting updates to 30 minutes or strategic planning sessions to two hours. This helps to prevent meetings from becoming unnecessarily long or frequent, both of which can lead to fatigue and decreased productivity. By defining limits, policies encourage organizers to prioritize key issues and use time effectively, ensuring that meetings remain purposeful and impactful. Additionally, guidelines for scheduling can prevent overlapping or redundant meetings, allowing employees to manage their time more effectively.

Company policies also ensure alignment with organizational values and priorities. For instance, policies may emphasize inclusivity by requiring that meetings accommodate diverse schedules, time zones, and accessibility needs. This could include providing closed captions for virtual meetings, scheduling sessions during core working hours, or offering recordings for those unable to attend. Such policies demonstrate the organization's commitment to equity and collaboration, reinforcing a sense of belonging among employees. By embedding these values into meeting preparation, companies foster an environment where every participant feels respected and empowered to contribute.

Another important aspect is compliance with legal or regulatory requirements, particularly in industries with stringent standards. Meeting policies may include mandates for documenting decisions, retaining records, or obtaining approvals to ensure compliance. For example, in industries such as finance or healthcare, where accountability and traceability are critical, company policies might specify how meeting minutes should be recorded and stored. Incorporating these requirements into preparation not only protects the organization from potential liabilities but also instills a culture of diligence and accountability among employees.

The role of company policies in meeting preparation is to provide a foundation for consistency, alignment, and accountability. These policies help to standardize practices, optimize time and resources, and ensure that meetings align with the organization's broader goals and values. By treating policies not as constraints but as enablers, companies can enhance the quality of their meetings and foster a culture of efficiency and respect. When embraced thoughtfully, these guidelines transform meeting preparation from an ad-hoc process into a strategic initiative that drives organizational success.

PRACTICAL FRAMEWORK: STEPS TO PREPARE FOR A MEETING

Preparing for a meeting requires a structured approach that balances strategic intent with practical execution. A clear framework helps meeting organizers ensure that every detail is addressed, maximizing the likelihood of achieving the meeting's objectives. The preparation process involves multiple steps, each contributing to the overall success of the meeting. By adopting a systematic methodology, organizers can create a seamless experience for participants, facilitating meaningful discussions and actionable outcomes.

The first step in preparing for a meeting is defining its purpose. A well-defined purpose provides clarity about what the meeting intends to achieve and sets the foundation for all subsequent preparation activities. Whether the goal is to brainstorm new ideas, make a critical decision, or deliver updates, articulating this intent ensures that every aspect of the meeting aligns with its objectives. This clarity also helps determine whether a meeting is necessary at all, as some objectives might be better addressed through other forms of communication, such as email or shared documents. By asking, "What do we want to accomplish?" organizers can ensure that the meeting has a focused and meaningful purpose.

Once the purpose is established, the next step is identifying the participants who need to be involved. Choosing the right attendees is crucial for productive discussions and effective decision-making. Organizers should consider who has the knowledge, expertise, or authority necessary to contribute to the meeting's goals. Inviting too few participants can result in limited input, while including too many can lead to inefficiency and distraction. Additionally, it is important to communicate the reason for each person's inclusion, ensuring that all participants understand their roles and responsibilities. This alignment not only fosters engagement but also helps attendees prepare adequately.

Developing a detailed agenda is the third step in the framework. The agenda acts as a roadmap for the meeting, organizing topics in a logical sequence and allocating time for each discussion point. A well-structured agenda includes the meeting's objective, a list of topics to be covered, the time allotted for each, and the roles of participants, such as presenters or facilitators. Sharing the agenda with attendees well in advance allows them to prepare and align their contributions with the meeting's goals. A thoughtful agenda ensures that discussions remain focused and time is used efficiently, preventing the meeting from drifting off course.

The fourth step involves preparing the necessary materials and logistics. This includes gathering and distributing relevant documents, reports, or data that participants may need to review ahead of the meeting. For virtual or hybrid meetings, ensuring the availability of technology such as video conferencing platforms, collaboration tools, and reliable internet connections is critical. In-person meetings may require reserving a suitable room, arranging seating, and organizing presentation equipment. By addressing these logistical details beforehand, organizers can eliminate potential distractions and ensure a smooth experience for all participants.

Confirming readiness through follow-up communication is an essential step in the preparation process. This involves checking in with participants to ensure they have received the agenda and materials and are clear about their roles and expectations. It may also include verifying the availability of resources, such as technology or facilities, to address any last-minute issues. A quick confirmation email or message can reinforce alignment and build anticipation for the meeting. This proactive communication demonstrates the organizer's commitment to a successful outcome and sets a positive tone for the session.

A practical framework for meeting preparation transforms a potentially chaotic process into an organized and intentional activity. By defining the purpose, selecting the right participants, crafting a detailed agenda, organizing materials and logistics, and confirming readiness, meeting organizers can create an environment that fosters collaboration, efficiency, and results. This step-by-step approach not only improves the quality of the meeting itself but also reflects a culture of professionalism and respect for everyone's time and contributions. To help implement this framework effectively, a checklist template can be a valuable tool, summarizing the key preparation steps. A typical checklist might include:

1. **Define the Purpose:** Clearly articulate the objective of the meeting.
2. **Select Participants:** Identify the individuals who need to attend and their roles.
3. **Craft the Agenda:** Develop and structure the agenda, including topics, time allocations, and responsibilities.
4. **Organize Materials:** Gather and distribute necessary resources, such as reports, data, or pre-reading materials.
5. **Confirm Logistics:** Finalize the details, such as location, technology requirements, or virtual meeting links.

To streamline these steps, tools like **Google Docs** or **Notion** can be incredibly useful for creating, editing, and sharing agendas collaboratively. These platforms enable real-time updates, seamless distribution to participants, and centralized tracking of meeting preparation efforts. Incorporating such resources simplifies the process, ensuring that every meeting is prepared with efficiency and attention to detail.

THE POWER OF THOUGHTFUL PREPARATION

Thoughtful preparation holds transformative power, turning meetings from routine obligations into impactful opportunities for progress and collaboration. It goes beyond checking logistical boxes; it is an intentional process that aligns participants, clarifies objectives, and paves the way for meaningful outcomes. In the professional world, where time and resources are limited, the value of deliberate and meticulous preparation cannot be overstated. It is the foundation that supports effective communication, fosters engagement, and drives actionable results.

One of the most significant benefits of thoughtful preparation is the clarity it provides to both the organizer and the participants. When a meeting is thoroughly prepared, it begins with a well-defined purpose that gives everyone involved a clear understanding of why they are there and what they need to achieve. This clarity minimizes confusion, reduces misunderstandings, and ensures that discussions remain aligned with the intended objectives. Participants who are given a clear sense of direction are more likely to feel invested in the meeting, knowing their time and input are being valued and utilized effectively.

Preparation also serves as a confidence-building tool, empowering both facilitators and participants to contribute at their best. For the facilitator, preparation ensures they are equipped to manage the meeting with authority, navigate potential challenges, and guide the conversation toward productive outcomes. For participants, receiving the agenda and relevant materials in advance allows them to enter the meeting feeling informed and ready to engage. This shared readiness elevates the overall quality of discussions, as attendees can focus on contributing thoughtfully rather than scrambling to catch up or adapt in real time.

Another profound advantage of thoughtful preparation is its ability to enhance collaboration and foster a sense of inclusion. By considering the roles, responsibilities, and needs of all participants, organizers can create a balanced environment where everyone feels empowered to contribute. Preparation might involve selecting diverse perspectives for a discussion, setting a tone of respect and openness in pre-meeting communication, or ensuring that logistical arrangements accommodate all attendees. These actions demonstrate intentionality, making participants feel valued and motivated to engage in collaborative problem-solving or decision-making.

The efficiency that results from preparation is another testament to its power. Meetings that are carefully planned tend to be shorter, more focused, and more productive. Time is allocated strategically, high-priority topics are addressed early, and unnecessary tangents are minimized. This structured approach respects participants' time and creates a culture where meetings are seen as purposeful rather than burdensome. Over time, such efficiency fosters trust among team members, as they come to expect meetings to be worth their investment of time and energy.

Beyond individual meetings, thoughtful preparation contributes to the broader organizational culture. When preparation is prioritized and embedded into meeting practices, it signals a commitment to professionalism and excellence. Teams begin to view preparation not as an optional step but as an integral part of collaboration and decision-making. This cultural shift elevates the organization's approach to communication, problem-solving, and strategy execution, creating a ripple effect of improvement across all levels.

The power of thoughtful preparation lies in its ability to set the stage for success. It turns what could be a disorganized or uninspiring gathering into a meaningful interaction that respects participants' time, leverages their expertise, and aligns their efforts with organizational goals. It is a practice that reflects intentionality, professionalism, and respect for the collaborative process. By committing to preparation as a non-negotiable element of meetings, organizations and individuals alike can unlock the full potential of their discussions and achieve outcomes that drive progress and innovation. To further enhance the impact of preparation, it is crucial to evaluate its effectiveness through post-meeting feedback. Tools like **Google Forms** or specialized software such as **Poll Everywhere** can be employed to collect insights from participants about the meeting's structure, clarity, and outcomes.

These tools allow organizers to create customized surveys that ask targeted questions about the quality of the agenda, the relevance of the topics discussed, and the overall preparation process. Gathering this feedback provides valuable data to refine future meeting preparations, ensuring continuous improvement. By integrating feedback collection into the workflow, organizations can close the loop on meeting preparation, transforming it into a dynamic and adaptive practice that evolves with the needs of the team.

Chapter 4: The Art of Facilitation

The facilitator plays a pivotal role in the success of a meeting, serving as the linchpin that holds the discussion together and guides it toward meaningful outcomes. Unlike a chairperson who primarily oversees formalities, or a presenter who focuses on delivering information, the facilitator's role is dynamic and multifaceted. They are responsible for creating an environment where ideas can flow freely, ensuring that the conversation remains productive, inclusive, and aligned with the meeting's objectives. By fostering a sense of structure and purpose, facilitators enable participants to engage effectively and contribute to collective problem-solving.

A skilled facilitator must navigate the fine balance between control and flexibility. While they provide the framework for the meeting, including the agenda and ground rules, they also need to adapt to the evolving energy and direction of the discussion. For instance, if a meeting deviates from its planned course but sparks a productive brainstorming session, a facilitator must decide whether to embrace this divergence or steer the group back to the original agenda. This balance requires a deep understanding of the meeting's purpose and the ability to discern which moments hold the most value for the participants and the organization.

Another key aspect of the facilitator's role is to act as an impartial guide. They must ensure that all voices are heard, particularly those of quieter participants who might hesitate to share their views. In doing so, they promote a culture of inclusivity and mutual respect, which is essential for fostering collaboration. This impartiality also positions the facilitator as a mediator during conflicts or disagreements, helping the group navigate contentious issues without alienating any member. By maintaining neutrality and focusing on the objectives, facilitators create a safe space for honest and constructive dialogue.

Facilitators also shoulder the responsibility of maintaining the meeting's momentum. This involves setting a clear trajectory for the discussion, keeping participants focused, and managing time effectively. Without proper facilitation, meetings can easily become sidetracked by tangential topics or dominated by a few individuals, leading to frustration and disengagement. A facilitator's ability to redirect the conversation when necessary, summarize key points, and clarify next steps ensures that the meeting remains purposeful and achieves its intended outcomes.

Ultimately, the role of the facilitator transcends the confines of a single meeting. A good facilitator leaves a lasting impact by modeling effective communication, collaboration, and problem-solving skills. Over time, their efforts contribute to a shift in the organization's culture, where meetings are no longer seen as obligatory time sinks but as opportunities for growth, innovation, and alignment. The facilitator's influence extends beyond guiding discussions; they inspire teams to see the value of coming together, sharing ideas, and collectively driving progress.

CORE SKILLS OF A GREAT FACILITATOR

The core skills of a great facilitator are foundational to the success of any meeting. These skills go beyond merely managing discussions; they encompass the ability to actively listen, guide conversations with purpose, and mediate conflicts with finesse. At the heart of facilitation lies the facilitator's capacity to remain present and responsive, ensuring that every participant feels valued and that the meeting remains productive. These skills transform a facilitator from a passive organizer into an active leader who fosters collaboration and drives meaningful outcomes.

Active listening is one of the most essential skills for a facilitator. It involves more than simply hearing what participants say; it requires a conscious effort to understand the underlying message, emotions, and intentions. Active listening creates an environment of trust, where participants feel acknowledged and respected. A skilled facilitator practices techniques such as paraphrasing to confirm understanding, asking probing questions to clarify points, and summarizing discussions to reinforce collective understanding. For example, when a participant raises a concern, an effective facilitator might say, "So what I'm hearing is that you're worried about the timeline. Can you elaborate on what challenges you foresee?" This not only validates the participant's input but also encourages deeper exploration of the issue at hand.

Guiding discussions effectively is another hallmark of great facilitation. This involves steering the conversation toward the meeting's objectives while balancing open dialogue with time constraints. Facilitators use questioning techniques to direct the flow of the discussion, such as open-ended questions to stimulate ideas or closed questions to confirm decisions. They must also recognize when a discussion has reached its conclusion and move the group forward without dismissing unresolved issues, often employing tools like the "parking lot" to capture side topics for future exploration. The ability to guide discussions ensures that meetings remain focused and that every participant feels their time is being used effectively.

Mediating conflicts is a skill that separates competent facilitators from exceptional ones. Meetings often bring together individuals with diverse perspectives, which can lead to disagreements or tensions. A skilled facilitator navigates these situations by maintaining neutrality and encouraging constructive dialogue. For instance, if two participants disagree over a course of action, the facilitator might intervene by summarizing both viewpoints and asking questions that guide the group toward common ground. "Let's take a moment to understand what's most important here. How can we combine these ideas to address everyone's priorities?" This approach diffuses tension and keeps the discussion solution-oriented.

Empathy is an underlying thread that enhances all of these facilitation skills. A great facilitator understands the emotional dynamics of the group and adjusts their approach accordingly. This might mean providing additional space for quieter participants to share their thoughts, acknowledging the frustration of team members when discussions stall, or celebrating breakthroughs to energize the group. Empathy enables the facilitator to connect with participants on a deeper level, fostering a sense of camaraderie and shared purpose.

The core skills of facilitation—active listening, guiding discussions, mediating conflicts, and exercising empathy—combine to create a powerful toolkit.

These abilities are not innate; they are cultivated through practice, reflection, and a commitment to growth. A great facilitator continuously hones these skills, learning from every meeting and adapting their style to meet the needs of their team. Through their expertise, they transform meetings from mundane obligations into dynamic forums for innovation and progress.

TECHNIQUES TO KEEP DISCUSSIONS FOCUSED AND PRODUCTIVE

Techniques to keep discussions focused and productive are critical for the success of any meeting. Without clear strategies, discussions can easily spiral into tangents, lose momentum, or become dominated by a few participants. A skilled facilitator employs a range of methods to ensure that the conversation stays on track and delivers meaningful results. These techniques are not only practical but also adaptable, allowing facilitators to manage the flow of discussions effectively in diverse contexts.

One of the most effective techniques for maintaining focus is setting and reinforcing clear ground rules at the start of the meeting. These rules might include guidelines such as allowing only one person to speak at a time, encouraging concise contributions, and adhering to the agenda. By explicitly outlining these expectations, the facilitator creates a shared understanding among participants about the conduct of the meeting. For instance, a facilitator might begin a meeting by stating, "Our goal is to finalize the project timeline today. Let's stick to this topic and address other issues in future sessions." Revisiting these rules periodically during the meeting helps to reset the group's focus when conversations drift.

Another key technique is time management, which is vital for preventing discussions from becoming overly drawn out or unproductive. Facilitators often use tools like time blocks, timers, or visible agendas to ensure that each topic receives adequate attention without monopolizing the meeting. For example, allocating ten minutes to brainstorm ideas and another ten minutes to evaluate them creates a sense of urgency and keeps participants engaged. When discussions threaten to exceed their allotted time, facilitators can use strategies like the "parking lot" method to table unrelated topics for later review. This approach allows participants to feel heard without derailing the meeting.

Effective summarization is another powerful tool for maintaining productivity. Summarizing involves briefly recapping what has been discussed and confirming shared understanding before moving to the next topic. For instance, a facilitator might say, "To summarize, we've agreed that the deadline for the first draft will be next Friday. Let's now discuss the resources needed to meet that deadline." This technique not only reinforces key points but also signals a natural transition to the next item on the agenda, minimizing the risk of backtracking or repetition.

Encouraging goal-oriented contributions is a technique that keeps discussions aligned with the meeting's objectives. Facilitators can achieve this by framing questions and prompts in a way that steers participants toward actionable insights. For example, instead of asking, "What do you think about this idea?" a facilitator might ask, "What specific steps can we take to implement this idea within our timeline?" This subtle shift in wording encourages participants to focus on solutions and next steps, making the discussion more productive.

Managing challenging dynamics effectively is crucial for maintaining focus. Meetings often involve participants with varying communication styles, some of whom may dominate the conversation while others remain silent. Facilitators can use techniques like round-robin participation, where each person is given an opportunity to speak, to balance contributions. Similarly, if a participant begins to monopolize the discussion, a facilitator might interject with a redirecting statement such as, "Thank you for your input. Let's hear from others who haven't had a chance to share their thoughts yet." By actively managing participation, facilitators create a balanced and inclusive environment that enhances the quality of the discussion.

Incorporating these techniques into meeting facilitation ensures that discussions remain focused and productive. By setting clear expectations, managing time effectively, summarizing key points, encouraging goal-oriented dialogue, and addressing dynamic challenges, facilitators can guide their teams toward achieving meaningful outcomes. These strategies not only optimize the efficiency of meetings but also foster a culture of purpose-driven collaboration.

Managing Dynamics: Encouraging Participation and Handling Disruptions

Managing group dynamics is one of the most challenging yet rewarding aspects of meeting facilitation. It involves creating an environment where all participants feel empowered to contribute while addressing behaviors or situations that disrupt the flow of the discussion. Encouraging participation and handling disruptions are interconnected tasks, both requiring skillful communication, empathy, and a firm but fair approach to ensure meetings remain productive and inclusive.

Encouraging participation begins with understanding the diverse personalities and communication styles within a group. Some individuals naturally dominate discussions, while others may hesitate to share their thoughts, particularly in a high-stakes or hierarchical setting. A skilled facilitator recognizes these dynamics and actively creates opportunities for quieter participants to voice their perspectives. Techniques such as direct but inviting questions—"Maria, I'd love to hear your thoughts on this"—can help draw out input without putting individuals on the spot. Similarly, structuring activities like breakout discussions or round-robin sharing ensures everyone has a platform to contribute. These approaches foster a sense of belonging and demonstrate that every voice matters.

Another effective strategy to encourage participation is to create a psychologically safe environment where participants feel comfortable expressing their ideas without fear of judgment. Facilitators can model this behavior by showing appreciation for all contributions, even if they challenge prevailing opinions or appear unconventional. For example, when a participant suggests an idea that seems impractical, the facilitator might respond, "That's an interesting angle. Can we explore how we might adapt it to fit our current constraints?" Such responses encourage open dialogue and signal that creativity and diversity of thought are valued in the meeting.

Despite the best efforts to create an inclusive environment, disruptions are inevitable in group settings. Dominating personalities, side conversations, and off-topic tangents can derail the discussion and frustrate participants. Handling these disruptions requires both tact and decisiveness. For instance, if a participant monopolizes the conversation, the facilitator might acknowledge their input before redirecting the discussion: "Thanks for that detailed perspective, John. Let's hear from others on the team to ensure we're considering all viewpoints." This approach validates the individual's contribution while subtly reinforcing the need for balanced participation.

Managing emotional disruptions, such as disagreements or conflicts, demands a calm and impartial stance. When tensions rise, the facilitator's role is to de-escalate the situation and refocus the group on shared objectives. One effective method is reframing the disagreement as an opportunity for collaboration: "It sounds like we have two strong perspectives here. Let's explore how we might integrate these ideas to find the best solution." This technique shifts the focus from confrontation to problem-solving, diffusing negativity and fostering a cooperative mindset.

In some cases, disruptions stem from external factors, such as technical issues in virtual meetings or distractions in hybrid setups. Addressing these challenges proactively is key to maintaining momentum. For example, establishing backup plans for technology failures or setting clear guidelines for in-person and remote etiquette can prevent common disruptions. When issues arise, facilitators who remain composed and solution-oriented set the tone for the group, minimizing frustration and keeping the meeting on track.

The art of managing dynamics lies in balancing the needs of the group with the goals of the meeting. Encouraging participation ensures that diverse perspectives enrich the discussion, while skillfully addressing disruptions safeguards the meeting's focus and productivity. A facilitator who masters these dynamics not only guides the group toward effective outcomes but also builds a culture of respect, collaboration, and shared purpose. Over time, these practices lead to more cohesive teams and meetings that are viewed as valuable, empowering experiences rather than obligatory tasks.

CASE STUDIES AND PRACTICAL SCENARIOS

Case studies and practical scenarios bring theory to life, illustrating how facilitation techniques can resolve real-world challenges and elevate the effectiveness of meetings. These examples provide valuable insights into the nuances of managing discussions, encouraging participation, and overcoming disruptions. By analyzing relatable situations, facilitators can refine their approach and gain confidence in handling diverse meeting dynamics.

In one scenario, a marketing team faced challenges during their weekly strategy meetings. The sessions consistently ran over time and often failed to yield actionable outcomes. Participants grew frustrated, feeling their time was wasted. Recognizing the need for a change, the facilitator introduced a structured agenda and time management techniques. Each agenda item was allocated a specific time slot, and the facilitator used visual cues to signal transitions between topics. Additionally, they summarized key points at regular intervals to ensure alignment. Over a few weeks, the meetings became more focused, with participants reporting greater satisfaction and productivity. This case highlights the power of structure and time management in transforming inefficient discussions into goal-oriented sessions.

Another example involves a product development team grappling with a dominant personality within their group. This individual often monopolized discussions, stifling input from quieter team members. The facilitator, observing this pattern, implemented a round-robin technique, where each participant was given equal time to share their thoughts. They also introduced anonymous idea submissions during brainstorming sessions to ensure that all perspectives were considered without bias. These changes shifted the team's dynamics, fostering a more inclusive environment where even the most reserved participants felt empowered to contribute. The case underscores the importance of managing participation to balance group dynamics effectively.

A virtual team meeting presents a different set of challenges, as illustrated in the next scenario. A cross-functional team spread across multiple time zones struggled with disengagement during their video calls. Participants frequently multitasked, and discussions lacked depth. To address this, the facilitator restructured the meetings to include interactive elements, such as quick polls and breakout sessions for smaller group discussions. They also encouraged participants to turn on their cameras and introduced a "check-in" question at the start of each meeting to build rapport. These small changes revitalized the meetings, improving engagement and fostering stronger connections among team members. This scenario demonstrates the importance of tailoring facilitation techniques to the unique demands of virtual meetings.

Handling conflict is another area where effective facilitation makes a significant impact. In one case, a project kickoff meeting between two departments became heated when disagreements arose over resource allocation. Sensing the rising tension, the facilitator paused the discussion and proposed a brief break. Upon reconvening, they reframed the conflict as an opportunity to align priorities, encouraging participants to articulate their underlying concerns. By focusing the group on shared goals and using a collaborative problem-solving framework, the facilitator guided them to a compromise that satisfied both sides. This case illustrates the value of emotional intelligence and reframing in resolving conflicts constructively.

A scenario involving a hybrid meeting highlights the challenges of balancing in-person and remote participation. In this case, remote attendees felt excluded from discussions dominated by those in the room. To address this, the facilitator employed technology to equalize participation, using features like hand-raising in the virtual platform and appointing a co-facilitator to monitor remote engagement. They also alternated between in-person and virtual speakers to ensure balanced contributions. Over time, this approach created a more cohesive and inclusive experience for all participants.

These case studies and scenarios emphasize the practical application of facilitation skills in diverse contexts. By learning from these examples, facilitators can better prepare for the challenges they might face and implement strategies to create meetings that are not only productive but also engaging and empowering.

Actionable Checklist: The Facilitator's Toolkit

A facilitator's toolkit is a collection of essential practices and strategies designed to guide meetings toward productive outcomes. This checklist serves as a practical resource for facilitators to prepare, execute, and follow up on meetings effectively. By breaking down the facilitation process into actionable steps, this toolkit empowers facilitators to stay organized, adapt to challenges, and ensure that every meeting delivers value.

1. Pre-Meeting Preparation

Preparation is the foundation of effective facilitation. Before the meeting begins, facilitators must ensure clarity of purpose, set expectations, and equip themselves with the right tools and information.

- **Define the Meeting Objective**: Clearly articulate what the meeting is intended to achieve. Is it to brainstorm ideas, make decisions, or provide updates?

- **Develop a Detailed Agenda**: Outline topics, allocate time for each item, and identify discussion leaders if necessary.

- **Select Participants Strategically**: Invite only those whose input is essential, ensuring the group is neither too large nor too small for the meeting's goals.

- **Communicate Expectations**: Share the agenda, objectives, and pre-meeting materials with participants well in advance.

- **Prepare Materials and Tools**: Test any technology (e.g., video conferencing software) and gather all necessary documents, presentations, or visual aids.

2. In-Meeting Facilitation

During the meeting, the facilitator must focus on guiding the discussion, managing time, and fostering an inclusive and productive atmosphere.

- **Set the Tone:** Begin with a clear statement of the meeting's purpose and a brief overview of the agenda. Establish ground rules to guide participant behavior.

- **Encourage Active Participation:** Use techniques like direct questions, round-robin sharing, or breakout groups to involve all participants.

- **Monitor Time Closely:** Keep discussions on track by sticking to the agenda and gently redirecting when conversations drift.

- **Summarize Key Points:** Regularly recap decisions and action items to ensure alignment and prevent misunderstandings.

- **Adapt to Group Dynamics:** Address challenges such as dominant personalities or conflicts calmly and constructively, maintaining focus on the meeting's goals.

3. Post-Meeting Follow-Up

The success of a meeting hinges on how well its outcomes are implemented. Post-meeting follow-up ensures accountability and reinforces the value of the discussion.

- **Distribute Meeting Notes:** Summarize key takeaways, decisions, and action items in a clear and concise format, and share them with all participants promptly.

- **Assign Ownership:** Clearly specify who is responsible for each action item, along with deadlines for completion.

- **Provide Feedback Opportunities:** Encourage participants to share feedback on the meeting's effectiveness and suggest improvements for future sessions.

- **Monitor Progress:** Follow up on assigned tasks to ensure they are completed and communicate any updates to the group.

4. Handling Common Challenges

Facilitators often encounter unexpected issues during meetings. A proactive mindset and a few contingency strategies can help address these challenges effectively.

- **Managing Tangents**: Use a "parking lot" to document unrelated topics for later discussion without derailing the current meeting.

- **Resolving Conflicts**: Maintain neutrality and encourage constructive dialogue to mediate disagreements. Reframe conflicts as opportunities for collaboration.

- **Engaging Disengaged Participants**: Ask open-ended questions or assign specific roles to draw in quieter attendees.

- **Dealing with Technology Issues**: Have a backup plan for technical difficulties, such as switching to phone calls or rescheduling if necessary.

5. Building Long-Term Facilitation Skills

Facilitation is an evolving skill set. Facilitators can enhance their effectiveness by reflecting on their experiences and seeking continuous improvement.

- **Solicit Feedback**: After each meeting, ask participants for input on what worked well and areas for improvement.

- **Reflect and Refine**: Review your own performance to identify patterns, strengths, and areas for growth.

- **Stay Informed**: Keep up with emerging tools and techniques for facilitation to stay adaptable and innovative.

- **Practice Regularly**: Facilitate diverse types of meetings to build versatility and confidence in managing different scenarios.

This actionable checklist is designed to guide facilitators through each stage of the meeting process, ensuring a comprehensive and effective approach. By consistently applying these practices, facilitators can transform meetings into valuable opportunities for collaboration, innovation, and alignment.

The Art of Facilitation

Facilitation is more than a set of techniques; it is a leadership skill that shapes how teams communicate, collaborate, and achieve results. As this chapter has shown, a skilled facilitator brings structure to discussions while fostering an environment where creativity and inclusion thrive. By mastering the art of active listening, guiding conversations with purpose, and mediating challenges, facilitators ensure that meetings are not only productive but also meaningful experiences for participants.

The journey to becoming a great facilitator is one of continuous learning and adaptation. No two meetings are the same, and each presents unique dynamics and challenges. Whether it is encouraging quieter participants to share their insights or diplomatically addressing disruptions, facilitators must remain agile and responsive, tailoring their approach to meet the needs of the group and the goals of the session. This adaptability is what distinguishes good facilitators from exceptional ones.

Moreover, facilitation is not an isolated act; its impact extends far beyond the meeting room. Effective facilitators influence organizational culture, setting a standard for communication, collaboration, and decision-making that resonates throughout the team. They inspire participants to view meetings as opportunities for growth and problem-solving rather than burdensome obligations. Over time, this shift in perspective fosters a culture where meetings drive innovation and alignment.

To truly excel, facilitators must also embrace reflection and growth. Every meeting is a chance to refine one's skills, learn from experiences, and experiment with new approaches. Seeking feedback from participants, observing group dynamics, and staying informed about emerging tools and techniques are all integral to becoming a master facilitator. The commitment to improvement not only enhances individual facilitation skills but also contributes to more engaged and effective teams.

In closing, facilitation is both an art and a science. It requires empathy, precision, and a deep understanding of group dynamics. By applying the strategies outlined in this chapter and building on them with experience, facilitators can transform meetings into dynamic, results-driven forums that unlock the full potential of their teams. The art of facilitation is ultimately about creating a space where ideas converge, collaboration flourishes, and meaningful progress is made.

Chapter 5: Building Engagement and Collaboration

Engagement is the lifeblood of effective meetings, serving as the key to turning routine discussions into meaningful exchanges of ideas. Without engagement, meetings often devolve into dull, obligatory events where participants passively endure the proceedings, offering little input and deriving even less value. The distinction between mere attendance and active participation is profound, influencing not only the productivity of the meeting itself but also the cohesion and motivation of the team. When participants are genuinely engaged, their collective energy drives creativity, problem-solving, and decision-making, which ultimately translate into better outcomes for the organization.

The challenges posed by disengagement are manifold and deeply interconnected. A disengaged participant is not just an individual issue—it creates a ripple effect that undermines the entire team's productivity. When attendees are uninterested or distracted, discussions lose focus, decisions are delayed, and innovative ideas are left unspoken. This, in turn, leads to frustration among team members who are eager to contribute, creating a sense of imbalance and resentment. Over time, such disengagement can erode trust, diminish morale, and even prompt key contributors to question the value of collaboration. The cost of such dynamics is far-reaching, affecting not only the effectiveness of individual meetings but also the broader organizational culture.

Effective engagement requires deliberate effort and planning, starting with an understanding of why people become disengaged in the first place. Often, participants withdraw because meetings lack clear objectives, run longer than necessary, or fail to consider the unique contributions each individual can offer. Similarly, when facilitators dominate the conversation or allow certain voices to overshadow others, it sends an implicit message that some perspectives are less valuable. Addressing these issues begins with recognizing that engagement is not a one-size-fits-all solution—it must be tailored to the needs of the participants, the purpose of the meeting, and the context of the discussion.

Beyond its practical implications, engagement is fundamentally about fostering a sense of connection and ownership among participants. When individuals feel that their presence and input matter, they are more likely to invest themselves in the conversation. This requires creating an environment where ideas are not only welcomed but actively solicited and valued. Encouraging this level of investment transforms meetings from transactional exchanges into collaborative experiences where everyone has a stake in the outcome. Engagement, therefore, is as much about emotional and psychological alignment as it is about meeting logistics.

The success of any meeting depends on how effectively it taps into the potential of its participants. This means that fostering engagement is not a peripheral consideration; it is a central responsibility of anyone who organizes or facilitates meetings. It demands a commitment to thoughtful preparation, inclusive practices, and a genuine belief in the power of collaboration. As this chapter unfolds, it will explore the strategies, techniques, and mindsets that make meaningful engagement possible, transforming meetings into spaces where teams can thrive.

STRATEGIES TO ENCOURAGE ACTIVE PARTICIPATION

Active participation is a cornerstone of productive meetings, ensuring that discussions are not just one-sided lectures but dynamic interactions that harness the collective intelligence of the group. However, participation doesn't happen by accident; it requires intentional strategies that invite, motivate, and empower attendees to contribute. A crucial first step is setting clear expectations before the meeting even begins. By sharing the purpose, objectives, and agenda with participants in advance, organizers provide a framework that allows attendees to prepare meaningful input. When participants understand what is expected of them, they are far more likely to come ready to engage, knowing their contributions will align with the meeting's goals.

Creating interactive formats is another effective strategy for fostering participation. Traditional meetings often rely on long monologues or linear presentations, which can alienate participants. Instead, incorporating activities like brainstorming sessions, breakout discussions, or structured Q&A rounds can energize attendees and keep them engaged. For example, asking open-ended questions during the meeting encourages creative thinking and invites diverse perspectives. Interactive tools such as whiteboards or digital collaboration platforms can also add a layer of engagement, particularly in virtual settings, by giving participants a hands-on role in shaping discussions. These formats ensure that meetings remain dynamic, making it difficult for attendees to disengage or adopt a passive role.

Assigning specific roles to participants is a practical way to involve everyone meaningfully. Roles such as a timekeeper, discussion leader, or note-taker not only distribute responsibilities but also create a sense of accountability. When individuals have a defined task within the meeting, they are naturally more invested in its progress and outcome. Role assignments can also foster a sense of ownership, particularly when participants are given responsibilities that align with their strengths or expertise. This approach signals that every attendee is essential to the meeting's success, enhancing both engagement and productivity.

Another powerful method to encourage participation is to foster an environment of open invitation and inclusivity. This involves actively inviting opinions, questions, and ideas from all attendees, especially those who may be hesitant to speak up. Simple practices like pausing to ask, "Does anyone have thoughts on this?" or explicitly seeking input from quieter members can make a significant difference. Recognizing and validating contributions, even if they deviate from the main discussion, further encourages participants to share their views. This culture of openness not only boosts participation but also promotes trust and collaboration among team members.

Lastly, it's important to remember that active participation thrives on a balance between structure and spontaneity. While a well-prepared agenda is critical, facilitators must also allow room for organic discussions and unexpected insights. Encouraging participants to bring their unique perspectives or highlight issues not originally on the agenda can lead to valuable breakthroughs. This flexibility shows that the meeting is a shared endeavor rather than a rigidly controlled process, motivating attendees to fully engage. By combining clear expectations, interactive formats, defined roles, and a welcoming atmosphere, meetings can be transformed into collaborative hubs of active and meaningful participation.

USING INCLUSIVE COMMUNICATION TECHNIQUES

Inclusive communication is the foundation of meetings that foster genuine collaboration, ensuring that every participant feels valued, heard, and empowered to contribute. At its core, inclusive communication recognizes that diverse voices and perspectives enrich discussions and lead to better decision-making. However, achieving inclusivity requires deliberate techniques that create a safe and equitable space for all participants. This begins with active listening, a skill that demonstrates respect and attention to the speaker. When facilitators and participants actively listen—paraphrasing key points, asking clarifying questions, and affirming the speaker's contributions—they signal that each perspective matters. Such practices not only encourage more input but also build a culture of mutual respect within the team.

A critical aspect of inclusive communication is encouraging diverse voices, particularly those that may be overshadowed in traditional meeting dynamics. Often, quieter participants or individuals from underrepresented groups may hesitate to speak up, fearing their input may be overlooked or undervalued. Addressing this requires proactive facilitation techniques such as round-robin discussions, where each attendee is invited to share their thoughts in turn. Another effective method is using anonymous idea submission tools, particularly in virtual meetings, to ensure all perspectives are considered without bias. By actively creating opportunities for everyone to contribute, meetings become a forum for collective problem-solving rather than a platform for dominant personalities.

Neutral and accessible language is another cornerstone of inclusive communication. Meetings can quickly alienate participants if they are filled with jargon, acronyms, or culturally specific references that some attendees may not understand. Facilitators should strive to use clear and straightforward language that is accessible to all, ensuring the discussion remains inclusive and understandable. Additionally, tone matters; an overly critical or dismissive tone can stifle contributions and create a hostile environment. Instead, facilitators should adopt a supportive and constructive approach, focusing on encouraging dialogue rather than shutting it down. This mindful use of language and tone ensures that communication remains inclusive and productive.

Handling disruptive dynamics is also essential for maintaining inclusivity in meetings. Dominating personalities, for example, can unintentionally silence other participants, creating an imbalance that undermines collaboration. Facilitators must tactfully intervene, redirecting the discussion to allow others to speak. Simple phrases like "Let's hear from someone who hasn't spoken yet" can effectively balance the conversation. Similarly, addressing disengaged participants requires sensitivity and understanding. Rather than calling them out, facilitators can re-engage them by directly inviting their input on specific topics or framing questions that draw on their expertise. These strategies help maintain a collaborative and respectful meeting environment.

Inclusive communication is about fostering equity and trust, ensuring that all participants feel their contributions are welcomed and valued. This requires a combination of awareness, adaptability, and empathy. Facilitators must be attuned to the dynamics in the room—both verbal and non-verbal—and respond appropriately to encourage collaboration. Over time, consistent use of inclusive communication techniques not only improves the quality of individual meetings but also cultivates a team culture that prioritizes respect, diversity, and shared success. Such an environment empowers teams to tackle challenges more effectively, driving innovation and growth within the organization.

Visual Aids for Inclusive Communication

Visual aids can serve as powerful tools to clarify and reinforce the concepts of inclusive communication, offering readers concrete frameworks they can apply directly to their meetings. By presenting key ideas visually, such as through flowcharts and comparative tables, facilitators gain actionable insights that are easy to reference and implement. These tools not only make abstract ideas more tangible but also serve as reminders during planning and facilitation, ensuring the principles of inclusivity are consistently applied.

A **flowchart illustrating the steps to foster inclusive communication** could start with pre-meeting preparation, emphasizing the importance of setting a clear agenda and sharing it with participants. The next steps might include active listening, facilitating balanced participation, and managing group dynamics, followed by post-meeting follow-up to ensure inclusivity extends beyond the discussion itself. For example, the chart could visually depict decision points, such as when to intervene with a dominating speaker or how to re-engage quieter participants, helping facilitators navigate complex scenarios.

In addition to a flowchart, a **comparison table contrasting inclusive versus exclusive communication styles** can provide readers with a quick reference for best practices. This table might highlight inclusivity-focused behaviors like using accessible language, inviting input from all attendees, and actively validating contributions, contrasting them with exclusive behaviors such as relying on jargon, ignoring quieter participants, or dismissing unconventional ideas. For instance, under "inclusive practices," the table could detail techniques like round-robin participation or anonymous polling, offering actionable methods that facilitators can adopt immediately.

By incorporating these visual aids, the chapter provides not only theoretical insights but also practical tools that readers can use to transform their approach to communication. Facilitators can use the flowchart as a guide to structure their meetings inclusively, while the comparison table acts as a checklist to evaluate and refine their communication style. Together, these resources make the concepts of inclusive communication actionable and accessible, empowering readers to foster collaboration and engagement effectively.

ROLE OF EMPATHY AND EMOTIONAL INTELLIGENCE IN ENGAGEMENT

Empathy and emotional intelligence are critical for creating meetings that are not just productive but also genuinely engaging for all participants. Empathy enables facilitators and participants to understand and connect with the emotions, perspectives, and needs of others, while emotional intelligence provides the tools to navigate these dynamics effectively. Together, they form the emotional foundation of meetings where individuals feel valued and heard, fostering collaboration and trust. Empathy begins with recognizing that meetings are more than just operational—they are relational. Every attendee brings unique insights, challenges, and motivations, and a meeting that acknowledges and adapts to these factors will naturally invite greater engagement.

One of the primary roles of empathy in engagement is building psychological safety—a sense that individuals can express themselves without fear of judgment or reprisal. When facilitators approach discussions with empathy, they create an environment where participants are more likely to share their ideas and concerns openly. For instance, acknowledging the effort or emotions behind a participant's input, even if it diverges from the topic, validates their presence and perspective. This sense of inclusion motivates individuals to engage more fully, knowing their contributions will be respected and appreciated. Over time, this dynamic strengthens team cohesion and fosters a culture of openness and mutual respect.

Emotional intelligence, meanwhile, provides practical skills for managing the complexities of human interaction during meetings. It includes self-awareness, which allows facilitators to recognize how their own emotions or biases might influence their behavior and decisions. By maintaining emotional control, facilitators can model calmness and fairness, even in tense situations. Additionally, social awareness—another component of emotional intelligence—enables facilitators to read the room, noticing subtle cues such as body language or tone of voice that might indicate disengagement, frustration, or hesitation. Responding to these cues with empathy and tact ensures that all participants remain included and engaged.

Empathy and emotional intelligence are particularly valuable in handling conflicts or disruptions during meetings. Disagreements are inevitable when diverse perspectives are brought together, but they need not derail the discussion. A facilitator with strong emotional intelligence can acknowledge the validity of differing viewpoints while steering the conversation back to the agenda. For example, saying, "I appreciate both perspectives; let's explore how they might complement each other" reframes conflict as an opportunity for growth. Similarly, empathetic facilitation addresses underlying tensions, such as stress or resistance, by understanding their root causes rather than dismissing them outright. This approach diffuses negativity and fosters constructive dialogue.

Beyond conflict management, empathy and emotional intelligence enrich engagement by personalizing the meeting experience. Recognizing individual strengths, preferences, and challenges allows facilitators to tailor their approach, ensuring everyone has a chance to contribute in a way that feels comfortable and impactful. For example, introverted participants may prefer written feedback or smaller group discussions, while extroverts might thrive in open debates. A facilitator who adapts to these needs creates a balanced environment where all voices are heard. By integrating empathy and emotional intelligence into their meeting practices, leaders can transform meetings from routine events into meaningful interactions that drive innovation, collaboration, and lasting engagement.

Self-Assessment: Evaluating Emotional Intelligence and Communication Style

To effectively integrate empathy and emotional intelligence into meeting practices, facilitators can benefit from a reflective self-assessment. This questionnaire is designed to help leaders evaluate their strengths and identify areas for improvement in fostering engagement and collaboration. By answering honestly, facilitators can develop greater self-awareness and refine their approach to creating inclusive and productive meetings.

1. **Self-Awareness**
    - Do I notice and understand my emotional state during meetings?
    - How often do I recognize when my emotions influence my behavior or decisions in a meeting?
    - Am I aware of my verbal and non-verbal communication and how it might be perceived by others?

2. **Empathy**
    - How frequently do I consider the perspectives and emotions of meeting participants?
    - Do I make an effort to validate and acknowledge the contributions of all attendees?
    - How effectively do I adapt my communication to accommodate different personalities and cultural backgrounds?

3. **Active Listening**
    - Am I fully present and attentive when others are speaking?
    - Do I ask clarifying questions and paraphrase points to show understanding?
    - How often do I interrupt or dominate discussions, rather than allowing space for others to contribute?

4. **Social Awareness**
    - Can I accurately read the mood and energy of the room during meetings?

- o How well do I notice non-verbal cues like body language, facial expressions, or tone of voice?
- o Do I take steps to address disengagement or tension when I sense it?

5. **Conflict Resolution**
   - o Am I comfortable mediating disagreements without escalating tensions?
   - o How effectively do I manage dominant personalities or redirect discussions to maintain balance?
   - o Do I encourage participants to focus on shared goals rather than individual differences during conflicts?

6. **Adaptability and Feedback**
   - o How open am I to adjusting the meeting structure or approach based on participant feedback?
   - o Do I actively seek input from attendees about how the meeting could be improved?
   - o Am I willing to experiment with new facilitation techniques to better meet the needs of the group?

Scoring and Reflection

For each question, rate yourself on a scale from 1 (rarely) to 5 (always). After completing the questionnaire, identify areas where your scores are lower and consider specific actions you can take to improve. For example:

- If you scored low on active listening, focus on pausing before responding and paraphrasing participant points in your next meeting.

- If empathy is a challenge, try initiating conversations with participants before the meeting to better understand their concerns or expectations.

This self-assessment is not about achieving perfection but about fostering a mindset of continuous growth. By cultivating emotional intelligence and refining your communication style, you can create meeting environments that not only drive results but also build trust, respect, and collaboration

Putting It All Together

Engagement in meetings is not the result of a single strategy but the cumulative impact of a thoughtful, integrated approach that combines preparation, inclusive practices, and emotional intelligence. At its core, creating engaging and collaborative meetings is about recognizing that every participant has unique value to offer and ensuring the meeting environment is structured to harness that potential. Achieving this requires a commitment to clarity, inclusivity, and adaptability, with each element reinforcing the others. When brought together, the strategies discussed form a cohesive framework that transforms meetings from routine gatherings into powerful engines of teamwork and innovation.

The process begins long before the meeting itself, with clear communication about its purpose and expectations. Setting the stage through detailed agendas, role assignments, and pre-meeting preparation ensures that all participants arrive with a shared understanding of their goals and responsibilities. This preparatory work not only reduces confusion but also sets a tone of professionalism and respect, signaling that the meeting is worth their time and effort. Combining this with inclusive practices during the meeting amplifies engagement, as participants feel that their contributions are anticipated and valued.

During the meeting, inclusive communication techniques take center stage. Facilitators must create a space where all voices are invited and appreciated, employing strategies like active listening, equal turn-taking, and neutral language. These practices ensure that discussions are not dominated by a few individuals but instead reflect the diverse insights of the group. At the same time, facilitators must remain flexible, adapting their approach based on the meeting dynamics. This might involve redirecting a monopolizing participant, encouraging quieter attendees, or shifting the format to address emerging priorities. By combining structure with adaptability, meetings stay both focused and responsive.

Empathy and emotional intelligence serve as the glue that binds these practices together, transforming logistical strategies into deeply human interactions. Facilitators who approach their role with empathy build trust and psychological safety, encouraging participants to engage authentically. Emotional intelligence allows them to read the room, respond to tensions, and maintain a constructive atmosphere, even in the face of conflict or disengagement. For example, recognizing when a participant appears hesitant to speak up and offering them a supportive opportunity to contribute can completely shift the tone of the meeting. These moments of thoughtful facilitation are often the difference between passive attendance and active collaboration.

The key to putting it all together lies in consistency and reflection. Building a culture of engagement doesn't happen overnight; it requires ongoing effort and a willingness to learn from each meeting. Facilitators and participants alike should take the time to reflect on what worked, what didn't, and what could be improved. Feedback loops, whether through formal evaluations or informal discussions, help refine the meeting process over time. By integrating preparation, inclusivity, empathy, and continuous improvement, organizations can cultivate a meeting culture that consistently drives productivity, innovation, and team cohesion. Together, these practices ensure that every meeting is a step forward toward shared goals and stronger collaboration.

REFLECTIONS AND NEXT STEPS

Engagement and collaboration in meetings are not merely desirable traits—they are essential to achieving meaningful outcomes and fostering a sense of connection within teams. The journey to creating meetings that matter begins with an understanding of the barriers to participation and a commitment to overcoming them through deliberate action. By combining clear strategies, inclusive communication, and empathetic facilitation, meetings can transcend their reputation as time-draining obligations to become opportunities for growth, innovation, and alignment. These principles are not isolated tactics but interconnected elements of a broader approach that prioritizes respect, equity, and purpose in every discussion.

As readers reflect on the insights and strategies explored in this chapter, it's essential to acknowledge that the process of building engaging meetings is iterative. There will be moments of trial and error as facilitators experiment with different techniques to find what works best for their teams. Some methods, like assigning roles or using interactive tools, might resonate immediately, while others, such as balancing dominant and quieter voices, may require more practice and finesse. The key is to remain open to feedback and committed to refinement, as engagement is an evolving practice shaped by the unique dynamics of each team and organization.

Actionable change starts with taking stock of current meeting practices. Facilitators should assess how effectively their meetings encourage participation and identify gaps where engagement falters. This might involve gathering input from participants, analyzing meeting outcomes, or simply reflecting on moments when discussions felt stagnant or imbalanced. Armed with this awareness, facilitators can begin to apply the principles outlined in this chapter, starting with small but impactful changes. For example, introducing an agenda that emphasizes collaborative opportunities or experimenting with inclusive communication techniques can quickly set a new tone for meetings.

Looking ahead, creating engaging meetings requires a cultural shift within teams and organizations. This means embedding these principles into daily operations, training leaders to adopt empathetic and inclusive practices, and celebrating successes that arise from improved collaboration. When teams see the tangible benefits of active participation—whether in the form of innovative ideas, stronger relationships, or more efficient decision-making—they become more invested in the process. Facilitators and participants alike should approach meetings as shared endeavors, where each voice contributes to the larger purpose and every interaction strengthens the collective.

The path to better meetings is a journey of intentionality, practice, and reflection. By prioritizing engagement and collaboration, organizations not only improve the quality of their discussions but also empower their teams to thrive in every aspect of their work. The tools and techniques presented in this chapter are just the beginning. As facilitators continue to refine their skills and adapt to their teams' evolving needs, they will unlock the full potential of meetings as a platform for creativity, problem-solving, and connection. With each step forward, they contribute to a workplace culture where every meeting matters.

Post-Meeting Reflection Prompts

To ensure continuous improvement in meeting effectiveness, facilitators and participants should engage in post-meeting reflection. These prompts are designed to help assess how well engagement was achieved and identify areas for enhancement. By taking time to reflect, teams can build a cycle of feedback and iteration that fosters increasingly effective and inclusive meetings.

1. **Facilitator's Reflection**
    - Did the meeting achieve its stated objectives? If not, what were the obstacles?
    - How well did I encourage participation from all attendees? Were there any voices left unheard?
    - Did I adapt my approach to address unexpected dynamics or challenges during the meeting?
    - Was the meeting atmosphere conducive to open dialogue and collaboration?

- What feedback, verbal or non-verbal, did I observe that suggests participants were engaged or disengaged?

2. **Participant's Reflection**
    - Did I feel comfortable sharing my ideas and opinions during the meeting? Why or why not?
    - Were the meeting's goals clear, and did the discussion stay focused on those goals?
    - How well did the facilitator manage the discussion and address different perspectives?
    - Was my time used effectively, and did I leave the meeting with a clear understanding of next steps?
    - What could be improved to make future meetings more engaging and productive for me?

3. **Team Reflection**
    - Did the group achieve a balance of contributions from all members?
    - Were any significant ideas or concerns overlooked during the discussion?
    - Did the meeting foster a sense of collaboration and alignment on shared goals?
    - What specific strategies worked well to keep the group engaged and focused?
    - Are there any tools, techniques, or practices we should try in our next meeting to improve engagement?

Using Reflections to Drive Improvement

After reflecting, facilitators can synthesize feedback and take actionable steps to enhance future meetings. For example, if certain participants felt disengaged, facilitators can implement strategies like assigning roles or using interactive formats to encourage greater involvement. Regularly incorporating these reflections into the team's meeting process creates a feedback loop, ensuring that meetings are consistently refined and aligned with the needs of all participants. By making post-meeting reflections a standard practice, teams reinforce a culture of collaboration and growth, ensuring every meeting continues to matter.

Chapter 6: Problem-Solving and Decision-Making

The success of a problem-solving meeting begins with its structure. A well-designed framework ensures that participants remain focused on the task at hand, fostering an environment conducive to critical thinking and effective collaboration. The absence of structure often leads to meandering discussions, wasted time, and unresolved issues. A structured meeting acts as a roadmap, guiding participants from problem identification to actionable solutions with clarity and purpose. This process is essential not only for maintaining focus but also for creating an atmosphere where innovative ideas can thrive.

Central to this structure is the initial step of defining the problem. Without a clear understanding of what is at stake, even the most productive meeting will struggle to generate meaningful outcomes. Defining the problem involves more than stating the issue superficially; it requires peeling back layers to uncover root causes and underlying factors. Techniques such as the "Five Whys" or root cause analysis can help teams delve deeper into problems, ensuring that the discussion is grounded in addressing the core issues rather than surface-level symptoms. This clarity sets the stage for critical thinking by focusing participants on a shared understanding of the challenge.

An effective agenda is another cornerstone of structured meetings. It should delineate clear phases, such as exploration, brainstorming, evaluation, and decision-making. Each phase should have allocated time to prevent discussions from becoming disproportionately weighted on any one aspect of the process. For instance, devoting too much time to brainstorming without leaving space for evaluation may lead to a flood of ideas without actionable outcomes. A structured agenda also includes identifying who will lead each phase, ensuring accountability and a sense of progression throughout the meeting.

Creating an environment that encourages open discussion is equally important. A structured meeting does not mean a rigid or overly formal one;

it should still provide participants with the freedom to express ideas and opinions. Encouraging diverse perspectives and avoiding the suppression of dissent are vital to fostering critical thinking. Techniques such as round-robin sharing, where each participant has an opportunity to voice their thoughts, or smaller breakout sessions can help generate ideas from all participants, including those who might hesitate to speak in larger groups.

Facilitation plays a crucial role in maintaining the structure of a problem-solving meeting. A skilled facilitator ensures that discussions stay on track, participants remain engaged, and time is managed effectively. They act as a mediator, resolving conflicts, addressing dominating personalities, and redirecting the conversation when it veers off course. The facilitator's ability to guide the meeting while remaining neutral is instrumental in preserving the integrity of the problem-solving process. Together, these elements—problem definition, a detailed agenda, open discussion, and strong facilitation—create a structured environment where critical thinking and solution-building can flourish. But how does this approach play out in real-world scenarios? To illustrate, consider the following case study of a company that turned a major operational bottleneck into an opportunity for innovation through structured meeting practices.

Case Study: Unlocking Efficiency through Structured Meetings
A mid-sized technology company faced significant delays in its product development cycle, with misaligned priorities and unclear task ownership among the primary culprits. The management team recognized the need for a more effective approach to their weekly project review meetings. They began by refining the agenda, splitting it into three focused segments: identifying critical bottlenecks, brainstorming potential solutions, and assigning action items. By clearly defining the problem and dedicating time for structured discussion, they encouraged open collaboration while keeping the meeting focused.

Facilitators also emphasized equal participation, ensuring that all voices, from senior engineers to junior developers, were heard during brainstorming sessions. As a result, the team identified several overlapping tasks that had caused confusion and delays. By implementing streamlined workflows based on their discussions, the company reduced its development cycle by 20% within two months. This case highlights the transformative impact of structured meetings on addressing complex challenges.

Interactive Exercise: Evaluating Your Meeting Agendas
Reflect on the agendas you typically prepare or encounter in your workplace meetings. Ask yourself the following questions:

1. Are the objectives of the meeting clearly defined?

2. Does the agenda allocate specific time blocks for discussion, brainstorming, and decision-making?

3. Do participants have access to the agenda in advance, allowing them to prepare effectively?

Based on your answers, identify one change you can make to enhance the clarity and structure of your next meeting agenda. This simple exercise can help lay the foundation for more productive and solution-focused discussions in your organization.

FRAMEWORKS FOR COLLABORATIVE DECISION-MAKING

Decision-making in a collaborative setting requires deliberate methods that harness the collective intelligence of the group while ensuring outcomes are actionable and efficient. Without structured frameworks, decisions often fall prey to biases, indecision, or a lack of alignment. Implementing decision-making frameworks provides a clear pathway for groups to analyze options, evaluate their implications, and arrive at conclusions that reflect the diverse perspectives in the room. These frameworks are not merely procedural tools; they are essential for transforming group discussions into meaningful and strategic decisions.

One of the most widely used approaches is consensus building, a framework that prioritizes group agreement without forcing uniformity. Achieving consensus involves creating an environment where all participants feel their voices are heard and valued, even if the final decision does not perfectly align with individual preferences. The facilitator plays a critical role in this process, guiding the group to identify shared goals and areas of compromise. While consensus can be time-intensive, its value lies in fostering collective ownership of decisions, which can enhance team morale and commitment to implementation.

Another effective framework is the Multi-Criteria Decision Analysis (MCDA), which is particularly useful when evaluating complex options with multiple factors. This method requires the group to establish criteria for decision-making, assign weights to each criterion based on importance, and score options accordingly. For example, in selecting a vendor for a project, criteria might include cost, reliability, and scalability. By quantifying these factors, MCDA reduces ambiguity and helps the group focus on data-driven decisions. While this framework requires preparation and consensus on the weighting process, it is invaluable for decisions requiring transparency and rigor.

The Delphi technique offers a structured approach for collaborative decision-making that minimizes group dynamics and interpersonal bias. Originally designed for expert panels, this method involves gathering input from participants individually and anonymously, often in multiple rounds. After each round, the facilitator shares aggregated results with the group, encouraging refinement and deeper insights. This iterative process allows participants to build on each other's ideas without the influence of hierarchy or dominant personalities. The Delphi method is especially effective for complex decisions requiring expert judgment or when consensus is initially elusive.

One of the more creative frameworks is Edward de Bono's Six Thinking Hats, which encourages participants to explore decisions from six distinct perspectives, each represented by a metaphorical hat. For example, the "white hat" focuses on facts and data, while the "yellow hat" emphasizes optimism and potential benefits. By guiding participants to think systematically from different angles, this framework minimizes cognitive biases and ensures a well-rounded evaluation. The Six Thinking Hats approach is particularly beneficial in meetings where creativity and innovation are required alongside analytical rigor.

Selecting the right decision-making framework depends on the objectives of the meeting, the complexity of the decision, and the dynamics of the group. For straightforward decisions, simpler methods like consensus building may suffice, while more intricate choices might call for tools like MCDA or the Delphi technique. Ultimately, the chosen framework should align with the meeting's goals, enabling the group to navigate complexity and reach decisions that are both effective and actionable. Through thoughtful use of these frameworks, meetings can become strategic opportunities to solve problems collaboratively and make decisions that drive meaningful progress. To bring these concepts to life and make them actionable, it is helpful to visualize the process and have practical tools at your disposal for implementation.

Visual Aid: Understanding Decision-Making Frameworks

Imagine a team tasked with choosing a new software platform for their organization. Using the **Multi-Criteria Decision Analysis (MCDA)** framework, the team begins by identifying key evaluation criteria such as cost, ease of use, and scalability. They assign weights to each criterion based on its importance and then score each software option accordingly. A diagram illustrating this process—complete with sample weights and scores—can help readers visualize how MCDA transforms subjective preferences into objective, data-driven decisions. Similarly, for **Six Thinking Hats**, a flowchart showing how participants alternate between perspectives like logical (white hat) and creative (green hat) thinking can demystify the approach and encourage adoption.

Practical Tip: Framework Templates for Immediate Use

To support readers in applying these methods, templates can simplify the process. For instance, a **scoring sheet for MCDA** might include columns for criteria, weights, and scores for each option, with a total score at the bottom for easy comparison. For the **Delphi technique**, a set of sample prompts could guide facilitators in designing anonymous input rounds, such as "What are the top three risks you foresee in this strategy?" or "Suggest two alternative solutions to this challenge." These templates provide a starting point for readers to incorporate structured frameworks into their meetings without needing extensive preparation.

By combining visual aids with practical tools, decision-making frameworks become accessible and actionable, equipping teams with the clarity and confidence to tackle even the most complex challenges collaboratively.

AVOIDING GROUPTHINK AND BALANCING DIVERSE PERSPECTIVES

Groupthink is one of the most insidious barriers to effective decision-making in meetings. It occurs when the desire for harmony or conformity within a group overrides critical evaluation, leading to poor decisions that fail to account for alternative viewpoints. Symptoms of groupthink include the suppression of dissent, overconfidence in the group's conclusions, and a tendency to ignore potential risks. Historically, some of the most notable organizational failures, such as the Challenger space shuttle disaster, have been attributed to groupthink. Recognizing and actively preventing this phenomenon is essential to ensuring robust and inclusive decision-making processes.

A key strategy for avoiding groupthink is fostering an environment that encourages dissent and critical evaluation. This begins with the meeting facilitator, who must emphasize that all opinions are valuable and that disagreements are not only acceptable but encouraged. Assigning a "devil's advocate" is a particularly effective tactic. This role involves someone intentionally challenging ideas, presenting alternative viewpoints, or questioning assumptions to test the resilience of proposed solutions. By normalizing such challenges, groups can maintain a culture of constructive scrutiny without personal conflict.

Anonymity can also be a powerful tool in preventing groupthink. When individuals feel safe to express their thoughts without fear of judgment, they are more likely to share candid feedback or unconventional ideas. This can be achieved through tools like anonymous surveys, polling software, or suggestion boxes integrated into the meeting process. These methods help level the playing field, particularly in hierarchically structured groups, where junior members might otherwise hesitate to voice dissenting opinions in front of senior leaders. Anonymous input ensures that ideas are judged on their merit rather than the status of the individual proposing them.

Balancing diverse perspectives goes hand in hand with combating groupthink. Meetings are at their most effective when they bring together individuals with varied expertise, experiences, and viewpoints. However, simply having a diverse group is not enough; active effort must be made to ensure that all voices are heard. One approach is to structure the meeting to include dedicated time for input from every participant. Facilitators can directly ask quieter members for their thoughts or use structured activities like round-robin discussions to give everyone an opportunity to contribute. This not only enriches the discussion but also helps participants feel valued and engaged.

Emotional intelligence plays a significant role in managing and balancing diverse perspectives. The facilitator must be attuned to group dynamics, identifying when certain voices are dominating or when others are being marginalized. Intervening tactfully to redirect the conversation or validate quieter participants is crucial. Additionally, the use of empathy can help the group navigate disagreements constructively. For instance, acknowledging the validity of differing opinions before seeking common ground can defuse tension and foster a sense of collaboration.

By actively combating groupthink and cultivating an inclusive environment, meetings can harness the full potential of their participants. These efforts not only lead to more robust decision-making but also foster a culture of trust and respect, where individuals feel confident sharing their ideas. In the long term, this balance of perspectives strengthens team cohesion and enhances the quality of organizational outcomes. Through vigilance and deliberate strategies, meetings can become platforms where diverse ideas converge to generate innovative and effective solutions. To further explore this dynamic, it is valuable to examine the consequences of neglecting these principles and to consider practical tools and exercises that can help teams stay on the right track.

Case Study: The Cost of Groupthink in Organizational Decisions
One of the most notable examples of groupthink occurred during the planning of the Challenger space shuttle launch in 1986. Despite warnings from engineers about the potential for catastrophic failure due to low temperatures affecting the shuttle's O-rings, decision-makers prioritized maintaining the schedule and dismissed dissenting opinions. This pressure to conform and avoid conflict led to the tragic loss of the shuttle and its crew. The Challenger disaster serves as a sobering reminder of the dangers of suppressing diverse perspectives and the importance of fostering open, critical discussions in decision-making forums.

Tool: Leveraging Anonymous Input to Encourage Openness
To counteract the pressures of groupthink, teams can benefit from using anonymous input tools, such as platforms like **Slido, Poll Everywhere**, or **Mentimeter**. These apps allow participants to submit ideas, feedback, or votes without attribution, ensuring that contributions are evaluated on merit rather than the individual presenting them. Facilitators can use these tools to gather honest insights on contentious issues or encourage suggestions from team members who might be reluctant to speak up in a group setting.

Interactive Exercise: Spotting and Countering Groupthink

Consider your own team or organization. Reflect on recent meetings where a decision was made, and ask yourself the following:

1. Were there any dissenting voices, or did everyone seem to agree too quickly?
2. Did the group fully evaluate alternative options or risks before deciding?
3. Were any concerns dismissed without thorough discussion?

Based on your answers, identify one symptom of groupthink you may have encountered and brainstorm at least two strategies to counteract it in the future. These could include designating a devil's advocate, using anonymous input tools, or actively seeking opinions from quieter team members. This exercise helps teams remain vigilant against groupthink and create a culture where diverse ideas and constructive debate thrive.

TURNING DISCUSSIONS INTO DECISIONS

As this chapter draws to a close, it's essential to reflect on the transformative potential of well-structured meetings as engines for critical thinking, problem-solving, and collaborative decision-making. By integrating structure, frameworks, and diverse perspectives, meetings can move beyond mundane discussions to become strategic opportunities that shape the direction of teams and organizations. Every meeting has the potential to be a crucible for innovation and alignment when handled with intentionality and care.

The tools and strategies outlined in this chapter—structuring meetings for clarity, leveraging proven decision-making frameworks, and fostering an environment that balances diverse perspectives—are not just theoretical concepts. They are actionable approaches that can be adapted to the unique challenges of any team or organization. A meeting's true value is realized not only in the decisions made within its timeframe but also in the ripple effects those decisions create across the organization. When critical thinking and collaboration are at the forefront, meetings become catalysts for meaningful progress.

The role of the facilitator, too, cannot be overstated. A skilled facilitator is not simply a neutral guide but an enabler of group intelligence, a steward of balanced participation, and a guardian against the forces of groupthink. This responsibility underscores the importance of preparation, mindfulness, and adaptability in ensuring meetings reach their highest potential. By fostering open dialogue and ensuring every voice is heard, facilitators help unlock the collective creativity and insight of the group.

Meetings are often dismissed as necessary evils of the workplace, but this chapter challenges that notion. They are opportunities—powerful, dynamic spaces where problems are dissected, solutions are crafted, and strategies are refined. However, realizing this potential requires intention and effort. The frameworks and methods shared here are not rigid blueprints but flexible tools that can be tailored to different scenarios, personalities, and organizational cultures. Their true power lies in their ability to transform meetings from static conversations into vibrant hubs of innovation and decision-making.

The success of a meeting is ultimately measured by the quality of its outcomes and the journey taken to reach them. It is a reflection of how well ideas were exchanged, decisions were made, and participants felt heard and respected. By embracing the practices outlined in this chapter, leaders and teams can turn meetings into moments of transformation, where problems are not just solved, but progress is forged. The next time your team gathers, let the discussions not just float in the air but crystallize into decisions that matter. To close this chapter, let us reflect on the profound impact effective meetings can have and inspire action by turning these principles into practice.

Motivational Insight: The Transformative Power of Meetings

Consider this: research by Harvard Business Review reveals that teams that use structured, inclusive, and goal-oriented meetings are 20% more likely to achieve their strategic objectives on time. This statistic underscores the power of purposeful gatherings to drive progress and innovation. As renowned author Patrick Lencioni puts it, *"If you run great meetings, your organization will become healthier, and your employees will be more productive and fulfilled."* Meetings are not just a necessary part of work; they are a cornerstone of organizational success when managed effectively.

Reflection Prompt: Committing to Change

Take a moment to think about the next meeting you will attend or facilitate. Reflect on the principles discussed in this chapter—structured agendas, decision-making frameworks, and inclusive dynamics. Which one resonates most with the challenges your team faces? Commit to implementing a single method in that meeting. Perhaps you'll refine your agenda to include clear decision points, use a framework like MCDA for evaluating options, or introduce an anonymous input tool to encourage openness. Small, deliberate changes like these can make a significant difference in the quality and outcomes of your meetings.

As you move forward, remember that transforming meetings is a journey. Each step you take towards more purposeful, inclusive, and solution-focused discussions brings you closer to creating a culture of collaboration and progress. Let every meeting be a reflection of the thoughtful, intentional leadership you bring to the table.

Chapter 7: Leveraging Technology in Meetings

Technology has fundamentally transformed the way meetings are conducted, reshaping professional communication and collaboration. In today's fast-paced business environment, technology offers tools that make meetings more efficient, accessible, and interactive. From enabling seamless remote connections to integrating collaborative features like real-time editing and polling, technology has bridged the gap between teams dispersed across geographies. However, while it offers immense potential, the integration of technology in meetings demands careful consideration to balance its advantages with the core human elements of interaction and engagement.

One of the most significant contributions of technology is the ability to connect people regardless of location. Virtual meeting platforms such as Zoom, Microsoft Teams, and Google Meet allow organizations to bring together participants from around the globe with just a few clicks. This accessibility ensures that meetings are not limited by logistical constraints, fostering inclusivity and diversity of thought. Furthermore, features like real-time transcription and live translation have made meetings more accessible to participants with varying needs, such as those with hearing impairments or language barriers. These tools have expanded the inclusivity of meetings in ways that were previously unimaginable.

Technology also plays a crucial role in enhancing productivity during meetings. Tools like shared digital whiteboards, screen-sharing capabilities, and real-time collaborative editing empower teams to work together effectively. For instance, project management tools integrated into virtual meeting platforms can streamline decision-making and ensure that action items are tracked and executed. Such integrations allow meetings to transition seamlessly from discussion to actionable outcomes. However, while these tools add value, the sheer number of available options can sometimes overwhelm users, making it essential to select the right tools aligned with the specific objectives of the meeting.

Despite its many advantages, the increasing reliance on technology also presents notable challenges. Technical glitches, such as poor internet connectivity or malfunctioning software, can disrupt the flow of meetings and hinder productivity. Additionally, the overuse of technology can sometimes lead to disengagement among participants. For instance, in virtual settings, the temptation to multitask or zone out is greater than in face-to-face meetings. These challenges highlight the need for a strategic approach to integrating technology, where the focus remains on enhancing collaboration rather than creating distractions.

The role of technology in meetings must be understood as complementary rather than a replacement for human interaction. The personal connections fostered through in-person or hybrid meetings are integral to building trust and rapport among team members. While technology can facilitate communication and streamline processes, it should not overshadow the importance of creating a space where participants feel heard and valued. The role of meeting facilitators becomes crucial in this context, as they must balance leveraging technological tools with maintaining the authenticity and depth of human connection.

TOOLS FOR IN-PERSON, VIRTUAL, AND HYBRID MEETINGS

The choice and use of tools can make or break the effectiveness of meetings, whether in-person, virtual, or hybrid. Each type of meeting benefits from different technologies tailored to its unique requirements, ensuring that communication flows smoothly and collaboration is seamless. Understanding the capabilities and limitations of these tools is essential for maximizing their impact while minimizing disruptions. By selecting the right tools and implementing them effectively, teams can elevate the quality of their discussions and drive actionable outcomes.

In-person meetings have traditionally relied on physical tools like whiteboards, flip charts, and projectors to aid discussions. However, with the advent of digital solutions, even face-to-face gatherings have become more dynamic and interactive. Tools like digital whiteboards such as Jamboard or Miro allow participants to brainstorm collaboratively in real-time while maintaining a digital record of their work for future use. Additionally, polling tools and audience response systems can provide immediate feedback, making sessions more engaging and participatory. These technologies not only enhance the clarity of communication but also ensure that ideas and insights are preserved beyond the duration of the meeting.

Virtual meetings demand a more robust technological infrastructure due to their dependence on digital connectivity and platforms. Leading solutions like Zoom, Microsoft Teams, and Google Meet dominate this space, offering an array of features designed to replicate and even enhance in-person interaction. From breakout rooms for small-group discussions to screen-sharing and recording capabilities, these platforms cater to diverse meeting needs. Virtual collaboration is further enhanced by integrated tools such as Trello for task management and MURAL for visual collaboration. These tools allow remote participants to contribute meaningfully, ensuring that distance does not dilute engagement or productivity.

Hybrid meetings, which blend in-person and remote participation, pose unique challenges that require sophisticated tools to bridge the gap between physical and virtual attendees. Smart technology, such as 360-degree cameras like the Meeting Owl or high-quality conference microphones, ensures that every participant, regardless of location, is seen and heard clearly. Platforms like Microsoft Teams Rooms are specifically designed to support hybrid meetings by synchronizing physical and virtual spaces, providing a unified experience for all attendees. Moreover, shared digital workspaces and real-time collaboration tools allow in-room and remote participants to interact and contribute on equal footing, fostering a sense of inclusivity.

Despite the abundance of options, choosing the right tools for each meeting type requires a strategic approach. The objectives of the meeting should guide the selection process, ensuring that tools are purpose-driven rather than overwhelming. For example, a brainstorming session may benefit from digital whiteboards and real-time polls, while a strategy meeting might require tools for document collaboration and in-depth discussions. Facilitators must also account for the technical proficiency of participants, ensuring that chosen tools are accessible and user-friendly.

The successful implementation of tools for in-person, virtual, and hybrid meetings depends on thoughtful preparation and clear communication. Familiarizing participants with the chosen tools in advance and conducting technical checks can prevent disruptions during the meeting. Additionally, providing access to resources, such as quick tutorials or support contacts, empowers participants to use the tools confidently. With the right blend of preparation, choice, and execution, technology can significantly enhance the effectiveness of any meeting format. To simplify the selection and application of these tools, the following infographics outline practical comparisons and mappings, offering a visual guide to choosing and leveraging the most suitable platforms for specific meeting needs."

Infographics for Tool Selection and Application:

1. **Flowchart: Selecting the Right Platform for Your Meeting Type**
   An infographic presents a decision-making flowchart starting with key questions:
   - Is the meeting in-person, virtual, or hybrid?
   - What is the primary objective (e.g., brainstorming, decision-making, information sharing)?
   - Are real-time collaboration tools required (e.g., whiteboards, document editing)?

   The flowchart directs users toward tools like Jamboard for in-person collaboration, Zoom for virtual group discussions, and Microsoft Teams Rooms for hybrid meetings.

2. **Comparison Chart: Features of Popular Platforms**
   A visual grid compares popular platforms like Zoom, Microsoft Teams, Google Meet, and Slack based on features such as:

- Scalability (small vs. large meetings).
- Integration with project management tools.
- Accessibility features (real-time captions, language translation).
  This infographic helps readers assess which platform aligns with their team's needs and technological capabilities.

3. **Mapping Tools to Meeting Types**

   A diagram groups tools by meeting type:

   - Brainstorming: Miro, Jamboard.
   - Decision-Making: Microsoft Teams, Google Workspace.
   - Status Updates: Asana, Slack integrations.
     The infographic visually emphasizes how tools cater to specific goals, enabling readers to make targeted choices.

By integrating these visual aids, organizations can navigate the overwhelming landscape of tools more effectively, ensuring their selection aligns with the meeting's purpose and participants' needs. These infographics provide a quick reference, streamlining decision-making and helping facilitators harness the full potential of modern meeting technology.

BALANCING TECHNOLOGY AND PERSONAL INTERACTION

While technology has undoubtedly enhanced the efficiency and scope of meetings, the human element remains a cornerstone of meaningful and productive discussions. Balancing the use of technology with personal interaction is essential to ensure that meetings do not lose the warmth, trust, and engagement that come from genuine human connection. This balance requires a mindful approach, where technology serves as a tool to support communication rather than replace it. Striking this equilibrium ensures that technology facilitates collaboration without diminishing the interpersonal dynamics that foster innovation and trust.

Personal interaction forms the backbone of effective communication, allowing participants to build rapport, express ideas clearly, and resolve conflicts constructively. Nonverbal cues, such as facial expressions, body language, and tone of voice, play a critical role in conveying emotions and intent. In virtual and hybrid settings, these nuances can be muted or lost, making it imperative to prioritize practices that maintain a sense of connection. Encouraging participants to turn on their cameras during virtual meetings, for instance, helps preserve visual engagement and creates a more personal atmosphere, even when people are physically apart.

One of the challenges of balancing technology and personal interaction lies in the potential for technology to create distractions. Virtual meetings, for instance, often come with the temptation for participants to multitask, check emails, or disengage from the conversation. Similarly, over-reliance on digital tools in in-person meetings, such as constantly referencing slides or apps, can detract from organic dialogue and collaboration. To counter this, facilitators must design meetings that integrate technology seamlessly into the flow of discussion, using it to enhance rather than dominate the proceedings. For example, incorporating short interactive segments like live polls or Q&A sessions can keep participants engaged without overwhelming them.

Facilitators also play a crucial role in creating an environment where technology supports rather than detracts from personal interaction. Effective facilitators guide discussions in a way that encourages every participant to contribute, regardless of the meeting format. In hybrid meetings, this might involve checking in regularly with remote attendees to ensure they feel equally included in the discussion. Similarly, facilitators can use digital tools sparingly, employing them at moments when they genuinely add value, such as summarizing complex points or visualizing data. By striking this balance, facilitators can bridge the gap between technology and human interaction.

Furthermore, integrating personal moments into meetings can help humanize the use of technology. Beginning meetings with casual check-ins or allowing time for informal conversations can break down barriers and set a collaborative tone. This is particularly important in virtual and hybrid meetings, where participants may feel isolated or disconnected. Simple gestures, such as acknowledging individual contributions or celebrating team milestones, can foster a sense of community and shared purpose. These practices remind participants that, despite the presence of screens or digital tools, they are still part of a cohesive team.

The goal is to leverage technology in a way that complements and enhances human interaction rather than overshadowing it. By prioritizing practices that maintain personal connections, facilitators can ensure that meetings remain engaging, productive, and meaningful. Technology should act as an enabler of communication, amplifying the strengths of human collaboration while addressing its limitations. This balance is not only vital for the success of individual meetings but also for cultivating a culture of trust and cooperation within the organization.

MANAGING HYBRID MEETING CHALLENGES

Hybrid meetings, which blend in-person and remote participation, offer organizations flexibility and inclusivity, enabling collaboration across locations. However, they also present unique challenges, such as ensuring equal participation, addressing technological disparities, and managing varying levels of engagement between remote and on-site attendees. Successfully managing these challenges requires thoughtful planning, deliberate facilitation, and the use of appropriate tools to create a seamless experience for all participants, regardless of their physical presence.

One of the foremost challenges of hybrid meetings is bridging the gap between in-person and remote participants. In-room attendees often have advantages in terms of visibility, ease of communication, and informal interactions before or after the meeting. Remote participants, by contrast, may feel disconnected, struggling to interject or follow the nuances of in-room conversations. To address this, facilitators must actively create a level playing field. For instance, using smart technology, such as 360-degree cameras and high-quality audio systems, can help ensure that remote attendees are both seen and heard clearly. Additionally, hybrid meeting platforms designed to synchronize physical and virtual interactions, such as Microsoft Teams Rooms, provide tools to equalize the experience for all participants.

Maintaining engagement is another significant hurdle in hybrid meetings. Remote participants may feel overlooked, while in-person attendees can become overly focused on their immediate environment. To counteract this, facilitators should adopt practices that promote inclusivity and active participation. Rotating roles, such as having remote participants lead certain segments of the meeting, can encourage equal involvement. Similarly, using interactive features like digital whiteboards or live polls allows both in-person and virtual attendees to contribute in real time, creating a sense of shared ownership over the discussion.

Technical difficulties, such as poor connectivity or malfunctioning equipment, pose additional risks to the success of hybrid meetings. A dropped connection or garbled audio can disrupt the flow of a discussion, leaving participants frustrated. To mitigate these risks, pre-meeting preparation is crucial. Facilitators should test all equipment and platforms in advance, ensuring they work as intended. Additionally, having contingency plans in place, such as backup devices or alternative communication channels, can help minimize disruptions. Organizations can further address these issues by investing in reliable, high-quality technology tailored to hybrid settings, such as adaptive microphones or cloud-based collaboration tools.

Hybrid meetings also challenge traditional facilitation techniques, requiring new approaches to manage the diverse needs of participants. Facilitators must balance their attention between remote and in-person attendees, ensuring that no group dominates the discussion. Simple practices, such as explicitly inviting input from remote participants or using visual cues like raised hands, can help ensure balanced participation. Establishing ground rules, such as asking all participants to mute when not speaking and encouraging video usage, fosters a sense of mutual respect and accountability across both groups.

Hybrid meetings highlight the importance of clear communication and shared expectations. Providing a detailed agenda and clear meeting goals ahead of time helps align participants, reducing confusion during the discussion.

Sharing meeting materials, such as presentations or key documents, in advance ensures that everyone has access to the same information, regardless of their location. Following up with comprehensive meeting notes or recordings further bridges any gaps that may arise during the session, reinforcing shared understanding and accountability.

Successfully managing hybrid meetings requires an intentional blend of technology, facilitation, and inclusive practices. By addressing the disparities between remote and in-person participants and fostering a culture of engagement and fairness, organizations can transform hybrid meetings into powerful tools for collaboration. This balance not only ensures that meetings run smoothly but also reinforces a broader sense of unity and alignment within teams. To illustrate these principles in action, the following case studies highlight organizations that have successfully navigated hybrid meeting challenges, leveraging innovative tools and strategies to create inclusive and effective environments for all participants."

Case Studies: Overcoming Hybrid Meeting Challenges

1. **Global Tech Firm Enhances Inclusivity with Smart Technology**
   A multinational technology company faced challenges in balancing participation between its headquarters-based team and remote employees across multiple time zones. By implementing smart cameras like the Meeting Owl and high-quality directional microphones, they ensured that remote participants had equal audio and video clarity. Facilitators used collaborative platforms like Microsoft Teams Rooms to create shared virtual workspaces, enabling both in-person and remote attendees to contribute seamlessly. Over time, the team reported higher engagement and improved collaboration in critical decision-making meetings.

2. **Nonprofit Adopts Role Rotation for Balanced Input**
   A nonprofit organization struggled with remote participants feeling excluded during hybrid meetings. To address this, they introduced a role rotation system where remote participants were assigned key

facilitation or notetaking duties for specific sections of the meeting. This approach not only gave remote attendees a sense of ownership but also encouraged in-room participants to focus on their input. By integrating this practice with shared visual tools like Miro and Google Workspace, the nonprofit successfully bridged the gap between the two groups, resulting in more inclusive and productive discussions.

3. **Startup Tackles Technical Disruptions with Pre-Set Protocols**
   A rapidly growing startup experienced frequent technical disruptions during hybrid meetings, often leading to frustration among team members. To mitigate this, the company established a robust pre-meeting protocol that included testing all technology, designating a tech support lead, and preparing backup platforms for critical meetings. These measures, coupled with the use of reliable hybrid meeting tools such as Zoom and collaborative project boards, minimized disruptions. The startup also began sharing meeting recordings and summaries to ensure continuity, even when technical issues arose.

These case studies demonstrate how intentional strategies and the right tools can transform hybrid meeting challenges into opportunities for stronger collaboration and alignment. By drawing on these examples, organizations can adapt similar practices to their unique contexts, ensuring their hybrid meetings are inclusive and impactful.

ACTIONABLE TAKEAWAYS

To translate the insights from hybrid meetings into practical, everyday improvements, actionable takeaways play a pivotal role. These takeaways serve as guidelines that leaders, facilitators, and participants can use to ensure every meeting is inclusive, engaging, and productive. The following strategies, grounded in the principles of effective hybrid meetings, are designed to address common challenges and create a balanced, seamless experience for all attendees.

Preparation is the cornerstone of success for hybrid meetings. Facilitators must go beyond the basics of scheduling to ensure all participants, regardless of location, feel equipped to contribute. Start by crafting a detailed agenda that outlines the meeting's purpose, key discussion points, and expected outcomes. Share this agenda in advance, along with any supporting materials, such as documents, slides, or pre-meeting tasks. Additionally, conduct thorough technology checks to ensure all equipment—both physical and virtual—is functioning correctly. This includes testing cameras, microphones, and conferencing software to prevent technical issues from disrupting the meeting.

Engagement strategies must prioritize inclusivity for both remote and in-person participants. Begin meetings with a quick round of introductions or check-ins to create a sense of connection. Throughout the discussion, use interactive tools like live polling, digital whiteboards, or Q&A sessions to encourage active participation. Hybrid meetings also benefit from clear facilitation techniques, such as explicitly rotating opportunities for remote and on-site attendees to speak. Establishing a "no interruptions" rule and maintaining clear conversational turns helps ensure that everyone's voice is heard and respected.

Technology, while essential, should be used to complement rather than overshadow personal interaction. Choose tools that enhance communication and collaboration without overwhelming participants. For instance, opt for platforms with integrated features like breakout rooms, collaborative documents, and shared visual aids to keep discussions focused and dynamic. Smart conference room setups, such as those with 360-degree cameras and adaptive microphones, can bridge the physical and virtual divide, ensuring a consistent experience. However, avoid overloading meetings with too many tools, as this can lead to confusion and disengagement.

Facilitators should also focus on creating a level playing field where remote participants are as visible and engaged as in-room attendees. For example, calling on remote participants for input or assigning them leadership roles for parts of the agenda reinforces their importance. When asking for feedback or making decisions, use digital polling tools to allow all participants to vote or provide input simultaneously, avoiding any perception of bias toward one group. Such practices foster a culture of inclusion and collaboration.

The follow-up process is critical to translating meeting discussions into tangible outcomes. After the meeting, circulate clear and concise notes that outline key decisions, assigned action items, and deadlines. Where applicable, include a recording of the meeting for reference, particularly for participants who may have encountered technical difficulties. Regularly revisit these action items in subsequent meetings to track progress and hold the team accountable. Gathering feedback on the meeting itself can also drive continuous improvement, ensuring that future sessions are even more effective and engaging.

Actionable takeaways for hybrid meetings emphasize the importance of preparation, inclusivity, effective technology use, and accountability. By integrating these strategies into their meeting practices, organizations can harness the full potential of hybrid setups, transforming them into opportunities for meaningful collaboration and alignment. Over time, these practices not only improve the quality of individual meetings but also contribute to a culture of excellence and engagement across the organization. To help implement these strategies effectively, the following checklists provide practical steps for ensuring hybrid meeting success. Whether preparing for a session, fostering engagement during discussions, or following up on outcomes, these guides offer a clear roadmap for turning principles into action.

Checklists for Hybrid Meeting Success:

1. **Pre-Meeting Preparation:**
   - Verify and test all technology (cameras, microphones, platforms).

- Share a clear agenda and supporting materials with participants.
- Assign roles (e.g., facilitator, note-taker, tech support).
- Prepare a backup plan for potential technical issues (e.g., alternative platforms).
- Ensure all tools are accessible to both in-person and remote attendees.

2. **Engagement Strategies:**
    - Plan interactive elements (e.g., polls, digital whiteboards).
    - Schedule check-ins to invite feedback from remote participants.
    - Rotate speaking opportunities to ensure inclusivity.
    - Encourage camera usage for remote attendees to maintain personal interaction.
    - Set clear ground rules for participation and minimize distractions.

3. **Post-Meeting Follow-Up:**
    - Share meeting notes with clear action items, responsibilities, and deadlines.
    - Provide access to the meeting recording for reference.
    - Regularly review progress on action items in follow-up meetings.
    - Collect feedback on the meeting's effectiveness to improve future sessions.

These checklists serve as practical guides, ensuring that hybrid meetings are well-prepared, inclusive, and outcome-driven. By following these steps, teams can address common challenges and foster a culture of engagement and accountability.

Chapter 8: Ensuring Accountability and Follow-Up

Follow-up is the bridge between conversation and action, transforming the ideas and decisions of a meeting into tangible outcomes. Without it, even the most productive discussions risk becoming exercises in futility. The process of follow-up ensures accountability among participants, fosters a culture of responsibility, and provides a clear pathway for achieving the goals set during a meeting. Organizations often overlook this crucial step, assuming that the momentum of the meeting will naturally translate into progress. In reality, without a structured approach to follow-up, the energy and clarity gained in the meeting room dissipate, leaving tasks undone and goals unrealized.

The importance of follow-up lies in its ability to clarify and confirm commitments made during a meeting. In many cases, participants leave with different understandings of the discussion, leading to confusion and misaligned efforts. Follow-up creates a shared reference point, documenting key decisions and assigning clear responsibilities. This clarity not only prevents misunderstandings but also empowers individuals to act confidently, knowing they have a roadmap to guide their efforts. When follow-up is neglected, ambiguity reigns, often resulting in wasted time, duplicated work, and unaddressed issues.

From a broader perspective, effective follow-up enhances trust and collaboration within teams. When individuals see that meeting decisions lead to real-world progress, they are more likely to engage meaningfully in future discussions. Conversely, a pattern of poor follow-up can erode confidence, leaving team members feeling that their input is undervalued or ignored. This erosion of trust has ripple effects across the organization, leading to disengagement and diminished productivity. By prioritizing follow-up, leaders signal their commitment to action and their respect for the time and contributions of their team.

Additionally, follow-up provides a framework for measuring the success of a meeting. A well-conducted meeting is not an end in itself but a means to achieve specific objectives. Through systematic follow-up, leaders can track the progress of action items, assess whether goals are being met, and identify areas for improvement. This evaluative aspect is essential for continuous learning and refinement of the meeting process. Without follow-up, it becomes difficult to discern whether meetings are driving value or merely consuming resources.

Follow-up plays a critical role in aligning team efforts with broader organizational goals. Meetings often involve decisions that have cascading effects on multiple projects and departments. Ensuring that these decisions are communicated clearly and acted upon is vital for maintaining alignment and coherence across the organization. Effective follow-up not only drives individual accountability but also integrates the outcomes of a meeting into the strategic fabric of the company. In this way, follow-up is not just a procedural necessity but a powerful tool for turning collective discussions into meaningful achievements.

DOCUMENTING DECISIONS AND ACTION ITEMS

Documenting decisions and action items is a fundamental aspect of effective meeting follow-up, serving as the bridge between discussion and execution. During a meeting, conversations can be dynamic and multi-layered, with numerous ideas, decisions, and tasks emerging. Without structured documentation, the energy and clarity gained in the meeting room can quickly dissipate, leading to confusion and missed opportunities. A well-documented meeting provides a reliable reference point, ensuring that all participants share a common understanding of what was decided and what actions are required. This clarity is essential for maintaining momentum and accountability.

The process of documenting meeting outcomes begins with capturing key decisions. These should be recorded in clear, unambiguous terms to avoid misunderstandings. For example, instead of simply noting, "The team will work on improving customer satisfaction," the documentation should specify,

"The customer support team will implement a feedback survey by April 15 to identify key pain points in the customer experience." This level of precision not only ensures alignment among participants but also creates actionable goals that can be easily tracked. A well-structured meeting minutes template can be a valuable tool in this process. Such a template should include fields for objectives, decisions, assigned tasks, responsible parties, deadlines, and unresolved issues. By using a consistent format, teams can simplify the documentation process while ensuring no critical details are overlooked.

Here is an example of a meeting minutes template:

Field	Example
Meeting Objectives	Identify strategies to improve Q2 sales.
Key Decisions	Launch promotional campaign in March.
Action Items	Marketing team to design campaign by Feb 28.
Responsible Parties	Marketing Manager (Emma).
Deadlines	Initial draft of campaign due Feb 28.
Unresolved Issues	Final approval process for ad budget.

A completed template ensures that every participant knows their responsibilities and the meeting's outcomes are formalized into an actionable plan. Visualizing this information in a structured way helps teams easily revisit and reference the agreed-upon goals.

Action items, a crucial component of meeting follow-up, should be outlined in detail. These items need to specify the task, the individual responsible, and a clear deadline. For instance, instead of broadly stating, "Review project proposals," the documentation should detail, "Alex will review the three shortlisted project proposals and provide feedback by March 10." This specificity eliminates ambiguity and ensures that tasks are both actionable and measurable. For longer-term projects or more complex tasks, integrating a visual aid such as a Kanban board or Gantt chart into the documentation process can provide added clarity. A Kanban board, for example, organizes tasks into columns such as "To Do," "In Progress," and "Done," giving the team a clear view of the overall progress.

Here's an example of how tasks might appear on a simple Kanban board:

To Do	In Progress	Done
Develop feedback survey (Lisa).	Draft campaign messaging (Tom).	Confirm Q2 ad budget (Sandra).

Such visual tools not only enhance individual accountability but also foster collaboration by making everyone's contributions visible. Digital tools like Trello, Asana, or Microsoft Planner allow teams to replicate these systems virtually, enabling real-time updates and seamless communication.

Beyond documenting decisions and tasks, it is equally important to track unresolved issues or follow-up questions. Not all topics can be fully addressed within a single meeting, and creating a section for open items ensures that these are not forgotten. Assigning ownership for addressing these issues ensures continuity and demonstrates a commitment to thoroughness. Combined with effective templates and visual aids, this approach to documentation lays the groundwork for actionable and accountable meeting follow-up.

STRATEGIES FOR EFFECTIVE FOLLOW-UP COMMUNICATION

Effective follow-up communication is essential for transforming meeting outcomes into actionable results. While the meeting itself establishes a foundation, it is the post-meeting communication that ensures decisions are implemented and goals are achieved. The process begins with a clear and timely recap of the meeting, typically distributed within 24 to 48 hours. This summary serves as an anchor for the team, reaffirming what was discussed and clarifying the next steps. Without such a communication, participants may lose focus, tasks may be forgotten, and the momentum generated during the meeting can be squandered.

The follow-up communication should be structured and precise, leaving no room for ambiguity. It should include a recap of the meeting's purpose, key decisions, and assigned action items, with clear deadlines and responsibilities for each. For instance, instead of stating, "The marketing team will work on campaign ideas," the summary should read, "The marketing team, led by Jane, will draft three campaign ideas by March 15 for initial review." This level of detail not only reinforces accountability but also provides a roadmap for participants to follow. A well-designed template for follow-up summaries can significantly streamline this process, ensuring consistency and comprehensiveness across all meetings.

Here is an example of a follow-up summary template:

Meeting Purpose	Align on Q2 product launch strategies.
Key Decisions	Finalized launch date: May 1.
	Agreed on primary marketing focus: social media.
Action Items	Marketing team to create social media calendar.
	Logistics team to confirm product inventory.
Responsible Parties	Marketing Manager (Sarah), Logistics Lead (Raj).
Deadlines	Social media plan due March 20; inventory report due March 25.

This structured format ensures that all critical details are captured and easily accessible. By consistently using such a template, teams can simplify follow-up communication and reduce the risk of miscommunication.

Visual aids can further enhance the effectiveness of follow-up communication. Tools like task trackers, Gantt charts, or dashboards can visually represent the progress of action items and help the team stay aligned. For example, a Gantt chart could display the timeline for tasks, showing how they intersect and depend on each other. Similarly, a Kanban board can categorize tasks into stages like "To Do," "In Progress," and "Completed," offering a snapshot of the overall status at a glance. These visuals provide clarity, making it easier for participants to understand priorities and monitor progress without needing to sift through lengthy reports.

Consider this example of a follow-up Kanban board:

To Do	**In Progress**	**Done**
Draft campaign ideas (Jane).	Create inventory report (Raj).	Finalize launch date (Team).

Such visual aids can be implemented using digital tools like Trello, Asana, or Microsoft Planner. These platforms enable real-time updates, allowing team members to check the status of tasks, post updates, or request assistance directly within the tool. Integrating these tools into the follow-up process creates transparency and ensures that everyone stays informed.

Regular updates are a vital component of follow-up communication, particularly for longer-term projects. These updates should be concise and focused, providing a snapshot of progress while addressing any potential obstacles. For instance, a weekly email might summarize completed tasks, highlight upcoming deadlines, and list any issues requiring attention.

Consistent updates keep participants engaged, maintain alignment, and provide opportunities to course-correct if needed. By combining structured summaries, visual tools, and periodic updates, leaders can create a follow-up system that drives accountability and ensures meeting outcomes translate into tangible results.

The tone of follow-up communication should be supportive and collaborative. While it is important to reinforce accountability, the follow-up should foster a sense of partnership rather than pressure. For example, instead of stating, "This task is overdue," a message might read, "I noticed the task is behind schedule—let me know if there's anything I can do to help move it forward." This approach not only maintains morale but also encourages participants to communicate openly about challenges. Thoughtful follow-up communication, supported by templates and visual aids, ensures that meetings do not end as isolated events but serve as catalysts for meaningful and sustained progress.

ALIGNING FOLLOW-UP WITH ORGANIZATIONAL GOALS

Aligning follow-up activities with organizational goals ensures that meetings contribute to the broader strategic vision rather than becoming isolated, tactical exercises. Meetings are often called to address specific issues or make immediate decisions, but their ultimate value lies in how their outcomes align with and advance the organization's priorities. Effective follow-up links the action items and decisions from a meeting to overarching business objectives, creating a direct pathway from discussion to impact. This alignment fosters a sense of purpose among team members, helping them see how their tasks contribute to the bigger picture.

To align follow-up with organizational goals, it is essential to frame meeting outcomes within the context of the company's mission, values, and objectives. During the follow-up process, leaders should communicate the "why" behind each decision and action item, ensuring that participants understand the strategic importance of their contributions. For example, if a meeting results in the development of a new marketing strategy, follow-up communications should emphasize how this strategy will support revenue growth, enhance brand positioning, or achieve other key business goals. By connecting tasks to high-level objectives, leaders can inspire greater commitment and focus among team members.

Another critical aspect of alignment is prioritization. Not all action items carry equal weight in advancing organizational goals, and effective follow-up should reflect this reality. Leaders must identify which tasks are most critical to achieving strategic outcomes and allocate resources accordingly. This prioritization should be communicated clearly to the team to ensure that everyone is focused on the most impactful initiatives. For instance, if a meeting produces a lengthy list of action items, follow-up communication should highlight the top priorities and provide a roadmap for addressing less urgent tasks. Such clarity prevents dilution of effort and ensures that the team's energy is directed toward meaningful progress.

Collaboration across departments is often required to fully align meeting follow-ups with organizational goals. Many decisions made during meetings have implications for multiple teams or functions, and ensuring alignment requires seamless communication and coordination. For example, a product development meeting may involve input from marketing, engineering, and customer support. Effective follow-up would include cross-functional updates, shared progress tracking tools, and mechanisms for resolving interdependencies. By fostering collaboration and maintaining alignment across teams, organizations can ensure that meeting outcomes are integrated into the larger operational framework.

Measuring the impact of follow-up activities is essential for maintaining alignment with organizational goals. Leaders should establish key performance indicators (KPIs) for meeting outcomes and track progress against these metrics during the follow-up phase. For example, if a meeting's purpose was to enhance customer retention, follow-up activities might include tracking changes in retention rates, customer satisfaction scores, or churn rates. By tying follow-up actions to measurable outcomes, organizations can assess whether their meetings are driving the desired strategic impact. This feedback loop not only ensures accountability but also provides valuable insights for refining future meeting practices.

COMMON CHALLENGES AND HOW TO OVERCOME THEM

The process of following up on meetings, while essential, is not without its challenges. These difficulties can undermine the effectiveness of even the most productive meetings if left unaddressed. Common obstacles include missed deadlines, unclear expectations, lack of engagement from participants, and over-reliance on key individuals. Recognizing these challenges and employing strategies to overcome them is vital for ensuring that follow-up activities deliver the intended results.

Missed deadlines are one of the most frequent hurdles in effective follow-up. Participants often leave meetings motivated but may become overwhelmed by competing priorities or unclear instructions. When action items are not completed on time, the momentum from the meeting is lost, and projects can stall. To address this, follow-up communication must establish clear deadlines, and leaders should check in regularly to monitor progress. Tools such as shared project management platforms can provide visual reminders of deadlines and foster accountability. Additionally, setting realistic timelines during the meeting itself ensures that expectations are feasible and aligned with participants' workloads.

Another common issue arises from ambiguity in responsibilities and action items. When tasks are vaguely defined or responsibilities are not clearly assigned, confusion can lead to inaction. For example, if a follow-up document states, "The marketing team will explore new channels," it leaves room for interpretation about who is responsible, what channels to explore, and when the task should be completed. Overcoming this challenge requires specificity in follow-up communication. Every action item should include details about what needs to be done, who is responsible, and the expected outcome or deadline. This clarity eliminates confusion and ensures that everyone knows their role in the follow-up process.

Participant disengagement poses another significant challenge. Some team members may not prioritize follow-up tasks or may fail to respond to reminders, leading to bottlenecks in progress. Re-engaging such individuals requires a combination of empathy and strategic communication. Leaders can start by understanding the reasons for disengagement—whether it stems from workload, lack of clarity, or insufficient buy-in. Addressing these concerns through one-on-one conversations or collaborative discussions can reignite commitment. Moreover, emphasizing the importance of each task in achieving larger organizational goals can help participants see the value of their contributions and stay engaged.

Over-reliance on a single individual to drive follow-up activities can also hinder progress. When one person is solely responsible for tracking tasks, sending reminders, and addressing bottlenecks, the process becomes vulnerable to delays if that individual is unavailable or overwhelmed. To counter this, leaders should cultivate a culture of shared accountability. This involves distributing follow-up responsibilities among participants, encouraging peer-to-peer check-ins, and using collaborative tools that allow all team members to track progress. By decentralizing the follow-up process, teams can build resilience and ensure continuity regardless of individual circumstances.

The challenge of sustaining momentum over time can be a barrier to effective follow-up, especially for long-term projects. Initial enthusiasm from the meeting may wane as new priorities emerge. To maintain focus, leaders should schedule regular updates or progress reviews that reinforce the importance of the tasks and celebrate milestones achieved. These reviews serve as checkpoints to realign efforts, address challenges, and maintain engagement. By proactively addressing these common challenges, teams can transform follow-up activities into a streamlined and effective process that drives meaningful outcomes.

QUICK TIPS AND ACTIONABLE TAKEAWAYS

Quick tips and actionable takeaways serve as the practical foundation for implementing effective follow-up strategies. These concise, targeted guidelines help individuals and teams immediately apply best practices to ensure their meetings translate into meaningful action. While the theoretical understanding of follow-up is important, simple and direct advice often makes the difference in ensuring follow-up becomes a consistent and impactful habit. By embedding these tips into daily routines, professionals can enhance accountability, streamline communication, and foster organizational alignment.

One key tip is to prioritize speed and clarity in follow-up communication. Sending a recap within 24 to 48 hours ensures that the meeting's outcomes remain fresh in participants' minds. A prompt summary should clearly articulate decisions made, action items assigned, and deadlines agreed upon, eliminating any potential for confusion. Delays in sending this information can lead to disengagement or misalignment, as participants may shift their focus to other tasks. Keeping the language straightforward and specific in these communications is equally essential, as it prevents misunderstandings and creates a shared sense of direction.

Consistency is another cornerstone of effective follow-up. Establishing a standard process for post-meeting activities ensures that no steps are overlooked, regardless of the meeting type or context. This process might include assigning a dedicated note-taker, using templates for meeting summaries, and maintaining a shared tracking tool for action items. A consistent approach not only simplifies follow-up but also builds a culture of reliability and trust within the team. Participants come to expect and depend on these follow-up mechanisms, which increases accountability and encourages active participation in meetings.

Proactively addressing potential roadblocks is also crucial. Challenges such as missed deadlines or disengaged participants are common but manageable with the right approach. For instance, incorporating a system of periodic check-ins ensures that tasks remain on track and allows for the early identification of obstacles. These check-ins can take the form of short emails, updates in a project management tool, or brief stand-up meetings. Leaders should adopt a supportive tone during these interactions, emphasizing collaboration rather than fault-finding to maintain morale and engagement.

Another valuable takeaway is the importance of leveraging technology to enhance follow-up. Digital tools like task management software, collaborative platforms, and automated reminders can streamline the process and reduce the administrative burden. For example, tools like Trello or Asana allow teams to assign tasks, set deadlines, and track progress in real-time, creating transparency and accountability. Integrating these tools into the follow-up routine ensures that critical information is easily accessible and reduces the likelihood of tasks falling through the cracks.

Creating a feedback loop to evaluate and improve follow-up processes ensures continuous growth. After a series of meetings, leaders should assess the effectiveness of their follow-up strategies, gathering input from participants on what worked well and what could be improved. This feedback can guide adjustments to templates, communication practices, or task management workflows. By iterating on these processes, teams can refine their follow-up practices, ensuring they remain effective and aligned with evolving needs. Quick tips like these, grounded in simplicity and practicality, can help teams establish a robust follow-up culture that drives consistent success.

Chapter 9: Measuring Meeting Effectiveness

Measuring meeting effectiveness is a crucial step in ensuring that the time, effort, and resources invested in meetings yield meaningful outcomes. In professional settings, meetings are integral to decision-making, team collaboration, and strategic alignment. However, without clear evaluation mechanisms, meetings risk becoming routine or, worse, counterproductive. Many organizations face challenges such as unclear objectives, disengaged participants, and lack of actionable results, all of which stem from unexamined practices. By measuring meeting effectiveness, organizations can turn these challenges into opportunities for improvement, creating a culture where meetings are not just events but valuable tools for achieving goals.

The primary reason for evaluating meetings is to ensure they align with their intended purpose. Every meeting should have a clear goal, whether it's making decisions, solving problems, or sharing critical updates. Measuring effectiveness through defined criteria allows teams to assess whether these goals are met. For instance, a strategic planning meeting should result in a documented plan with assigned responsibilities, while a project review might aim to identify bottlenecks and solutions. Without measurement, it's easy for meetings to deviate from their objectives, leading to frustration and wasted time. A structured evaluation process helps keep meetings goal-oriented and outcome-driven, ensuring they contribute to broader organizational success.

Another compelling reason to measure meeting effectiveness is the ability to foster accountability among participants and organizers. Meetings often involve multiple stakeholders, each playing a role in preparation, discussion, and execution. By evaluating outcomes, such as the completion of action items or the quality of discussions, organizations can hold individuals accountable for their contributions. For example, tracking whether decisions made during meetings translate into timely actions ensures that attendees are not just passive participants but active contributors to the organization's goals.

A data-driven approach to accountability also reduces the likelihood of recurring issues, such as unclear action plans or unproductive debates, by addressing them head-on with evidence-based solutions.

Additionally, measurement provides a pathway to identify and eliminate inefficiencies in meeting processes. Meetings are notorious for consuming significant time, often without delivering proportional value. Common issues such as overly long sessions, irrelevant discussions, or unnecessary participants can undermine productivity and morale. For example, a recurring team meeting that consistently runs over time may indicate poor agenda planning or inadequate time management. By gathering feedback and data, such as the percentage of agenda items covered or participant satisfaction scores, these inefficiencies can be addressed. Adjustments, such as introducing timeboxing or refining the attendee list, can lead to more focused and efficient meetings.

To illustrate the impact of measuring meeting effectiveness, consider the example of a mid-sized tech company that was struggling with disorganized meetings. Team members often left sessions feeling unclear about next steps, leading to delays in project delivery. The company introduced a post-meeting feedback process, asking participants to rate each meeting on clarity, usefulness, and time efficiency. Within six months, the feedback revealed that most issues stemmed from vague agendas. In response, the company implemented a standardized agenda template and trained meeting leaders on facilitation techniques. As a result, meeting satisfaction scores improved by 40%, and project timelines became more predictable.

Lastly, measuring meeting effectiveness is essential for fostering a culture of continuous improvement. When organizations regularly evaluate their meetings, they create a feedback loop that drives progress over time. For instance, a team might start by measuring basic metrics such as meeting duration and participant satisfaction, then expand to track more complex indicators like action item completion rates or stakeholder alignment. As these measurements reveal areas of improvement, teams can experiment with new strategies, such as adopting collaboration tools or changing the format of discussions. This iterative process ensures that meetings evolve in response to changing needs, maintaining their relevance and impact.

Measuring meeting effectiveness is not just a best practice—it is a necessity in today's fast-paced and resource-conscious professional landscape. By aligning meetings with clear objectives, fostering accountability, identifying inefficiencies, and promoting continuous improvement, organizations can transform meetings into powerful instruments of success. As the example of the tech company demonstrates, even small changes informed by measurement can lead to significant improvements in outcomes and satisfaction. With the right tools and mindset, measuring effectiveness turns meetings from potential time sinks into strategic assets that drive progress and collaboration.

KEY PERFORMANCE INDICATORS (KPIS) FOR EVALUATING MEETING SUCCESS

Key performance indicators (KPIs) are vital tools for evaluating the success of meetings, enabling organizations to move beyond vague impressions and take a structured approach to improvement. In a professional environment, meetings are expected to drive decision-making, foster collaboration, and align teams with strategic goals. However, without concrete metrics, it is difficult to determine whether these objectives are being met. KPIs provide a measurable framework that allows teams to assess the effectiveness of their meetings, ensuring that they are purposeful, efficient, and results-oriented. By tracking specific indicators, organizations can identify what works, pinpoint inefficiencies, and implement targeted changes to maximize the value of their meetings.

One of the most essential KPIs for meetings is **goal achievement**, which evaluates whether the objectives of the meeting were successfully met. Each meeting should have a clear purpose, such as solving a problem, assigning tasks, or aligning on next steps. Measuring goal achievement involves comparing the intended outcomes against the actual results. For example, if the goal of a planning meeting was to create a detailed project roadmap, the output should include a finalized plan with assigned responsibilities. By using this KPI, teams can assess whether their meetings are driving progress or falling short of expectations. To help readers apply this concept, a simple goal-alignment checklist can be included, prompting organizers to articulate the meeting's objectives beforehand and evaluate their fulfillment afterward.

Another critical KPI is **time efficiency**, which measures how effectively the meeting's duration was managed relative to its agenda. Time is one of the most valuable resources in any organization, and meetings that overrun or meander without purpose can disrupt workflows and lower productivity. Time efficiency involves tracking whether the meeting stayed within its scheduled time, whether discussions were focused, and whether participants felt their time was well-spent. For instance, a team meeting that consistently exceeds its allotted time may indicate a need for stricter agenda adherence or more concise facilitation. Including a template for time tracking, where organizers can record planned versus actual durations for agenda items, can help readers monitor this KPI and identify opportunities to streamline their meetings.

Participation metrics are equally important in evaluating meeting success, as they reflect the level of engagement and inclusivity among attendees. Effective meetings rely on the active involvement of participants, ensuring that diverse perspectives are heard and decisions are well-informed. This KPI examines factors such as the number of attendees who contributed to discussions, the frequency of interactions, and the balance of participation across roles. For virtual meetings, additional metrics like chat activity, polling responses, or use of collaborative tools can offer further insights into engagement levels. For instance, if data shows that a few voices dominate discussions, it may indicate a need for better facilitation techniques or structured formats, such as round-robin contributions. A sample participation heatmap, visually depicting who spoke and for how long, could be a useful resource for readers seeking to analyze and improve engagement.

Follow-up effectiveness is another key metric, focusing on whether decisions made during the meeting are translated into action. A productive meeting should result in clearly defined action items, assigned owners, and deadlines. This KPI measures the percentage of tasks completed on time and the extent to which outcomes align with the meeting's goals. For example, if a project review meeting identified three critical tasks, tracking their completion provides a clear indication of follow-up success. A recurring pattern of incomplete follow-ups might signal the need for better documentation or more explicit accountability mechanisms. Including a follow-up action tracker as a resource can help readers implement this KPI, ensuring that their meetings lead to tangible results.

Finally, **stakeholder satisfaction** provides a qualitative measure of meeting effectiveness by capturing participants' perceptions of the meeting's value. This can be assessed through post-meeting surveys, where attendees rate factors such as the clarity of objectives, the relevance of discussions, and the usefulness of outcomes. High satisfaction scores often correlate with well-structured and engaging meetings, while low scores can highlight areas for improvement. For example, if participants frequently report feeling disengaged, it may suggest the need for more interactive formats or better agenda planning. A template for a quick satisfaction survey, including questions like "How would you rate the clarity of this meeting?" or "What could have been done better?", can empower readers to gather actionable feedback from their teams.

To illustrate the importance of tracking KPIs, consider a sales team at a growing company that introduced metrics to evaluate their weekly strategy meetings. Initially, they found that discussions often strayed from the agenda, leading to extended durations and missed goals. By implementing KPIs like goal alignment, time efficiency, and participation rates, the team identified specific areas for improvement. Over time, they adopted more focused agendas, introduced timeboxing for discussions, and ensured that all attendees contributed to decision-making. Within three months, survey data showed a

35% increase in participant satisfaction, and the team reported completing 20% more action items after each meeting.

KPIs are indispensable for evaluating meeting success, offering measurable insights into whether meetings achieve their goals, respect participants' time, foster engagement, and drive follow-through. By incorporating tools such as goal-alignment checklists, time-tracking templates, participation heatmaps, and satisfaction surveys, organizations can empower their teams to systematically assess and improve their meetings. As the example of the sales team demonstrates, tracking KPIs not only highlights inefficiencies but also drives meaningful improvements that lead to more impactful and productive meetings.

CONTINUOUS IMPROVEMENT STRATEGIES BASED ON FEEDBACK

Continuous improvement strategies based on feedback are essential for transforming meetings from static, repetitive gatherings into dynamic and impactful events that consistently deliver results. Feedback offers a unique opportunity to understand what works, what doesn't, and how to refine the meeting process to better serve participants and organizational goals. When organizations treat feedback not as criticism but as a resource for growth, they create an iterative improvement cycle that keeps meetings aligned with evolving needs. This approach fosters a culture of learning, adaptability, and excellence, ensuring that meetings remain purposeful and productive over time.

The first step in leveraging feedback for continuous improvement is establishing effective mechanisms for gathering it. Post-meeting surveys are one of the most reliable tools for this purpose, allowing participants to provide structured input on various aspects of the meeting, such as agenda clarity, discussion relevance, and overall usefulness. These surveys can include a mix of quantitative questions—like rating the meeting's effectiveness on a scale of 1 to 5—and open-ended questions that invite detailed suggestions. For example, a question like "What could have been done differently to improve today's meeting?" encourages attendees to share constructive feedback. Incorporating feedback collection into the meeting process signals to participants that their opinions are valued, fostering trust and engagement.

Informal methods, such as real-time polling or a quick verbal debrief at the end of a meeting, can complement structured surveys. For instance, the facilitator might ask attendees to share one thing that worked well and one area for improvement. Tools like Mentimeter or Slido can be used to collect anonymous feedback during virtual or hybrid meetings, ensuring that even quieter participants have a chance to contribute. A practical addition to this section could be a template for a simple post-meeting survey, covering essential questions like "Did the meeting achieve its objectives?" and "Was the meeting length appropriate?" This ensures readers can immediately implement a feedback collection system tailored to their needs.

Once feedback is gathered, the next critical step is analysis. Isolated comments are valuable but often lack the context needed to drive systemic change. By aggregating feedback over time, patterns and recurring issues can be identified. For instance, if multiple surveys highlight that meetings frequently run over time, this suggests a structural issue, such as insufficient agenda planning or ineffective time management. Similarly, feedback that consistently points to disengaged participants might indicate a need for more interactive formats or better facilitation. Analysis transforms raw feedback into actionable insights, enabling organizations to prioritize the most pressing areas for improvement.

A compelling case study can illustrate this process. Imagine a marketing department struggling with inefficient weekly team meetings. Surveys revealed that discussions often veered off-topic, leaving critical agenda items unaddressed. Recognizing this pattern, the team introduced a new strategy: each meeting now starts with a review of the agenda and assigns a timekeeper to ensure adherence to time limits. Additionally, they adopted a "parking lot" technique to set aside off-topic issues for future discussion. Within a few weeks, survey responses showed significant improvements in both time efficiency and satisfaction. This example highlights how analyzing feedback and acting on it can lead to practical, impactful changes.

Acting on feedback is where the transformative power of continuous improvement lies. It is not enough to collect insights; organizations must implement changes based on the data and monitor their effectiveness over time. For example, if participants express that meetings lack engagement, facilitators could experiment with techniques like round-robin discussions, breakout groups, or interactive polls. Similarly, if feedback reveals confusion about action items, introducing a standardized follow-up process—such as sending a post-meeting summary with clear assignments and deadlines—can address the issue. To ensure success, changes should be communicated to participants, demonstrating that their feedback has been heard and valued. This transparency reinforces a culture of collaboration and trust.

The final step in creating a feedback-driven culture is maintaining a structured feedback loop. This loop involves four stages: collecting feedback, analyzing insights, implementing changes, and reassessing outcomes. For example, a product development team might collect feedback that brainstorming sessions feel rushed. In response, they extend the session length and adjust the agenda to focus on fewer topics. After a few iterations, they reassess by collecting new feedback, confirming whether the changes improved the process or require further refinement. This cyclical approach ensures that meetings remain adaptable and continue to improve over time.

Continuous improvement strategies based on feedback are indispensable for ensuring that meetings remain effective, engaging, and aligned with their objectives. By implementing tools such as post-meeting surveys, real-time polling, and feedback analysis techniques, organizations can systematically identify and address inefficiencies. Case studies like the marketing team's success with agenda adherence demonstrate the tangible benefits of acting on feedback, while feedback loops provide a sustainable framework for ongoing refinement. Ultimately, a commitment to continuous improvement transforms meetings from static events into dynamic opportunities for growth, collaboration, and organizational success.

ROLE OF DATA IN REFINING MEETING PROCESSES

Data plays a transformative role in refining meeting processes, providing the clarity and objectivity needed to ensure that meetings achieve their intended goals. In many organizations, meetings are viewed as necessary rituals but are often left unevaluated, leading to inefficiencies that go unnoticed. Leveraging data allows teams to move beyond subjective assessments and adopt a systematic approach to improvement. By collecting, analyzing, and applying data, organizations can identify inefficiencies, implement targeted changes, and track progress over time. This approach ensures that meetings evolve into strategic assets that drive decision-making, foster collaboration, and align with organizational goals.

One of the most valuable contributions of data is its ability to quantify meeting performance through specific metrics. Key data points such as attendance, duration, participation levels, and action item completion provide tangible evidence of a meeting's effectiveness. For instance, tracking attendance trends can reveal whether the right people are consistently participating in key discussions. Low attendance rates might indicate scheduling conflicts, unclear invitations, or a perception that the meeting lacks value. Similarly, participation data—such as the number of attendees actively contributing to discussions—can highlight whether meetings are inclusive and engaging or dominated by a few voices. Organizations can integrate these metrics into dashboards or spreadsheets for easy tracking, offering a clear picture of meeting performance over time.

Another critical aspect of data in meeting refinement is its ability to measure outcomes, particularly the implementation of decisions and follow-up actions. A meeting that generates ideas or decisions but fails to see them executed effectively wastes both time and effort. Tracking follow-up success involves monitoring metrics like the percentage of assigned tasks completed on time or the alignment of outcomes with the meeting's objectives. For example, if a product team consistently struggles to deliver on decisions made during sprint planning meetings, data on incomplete tasks could signal a need for clearer documentation or accountability mechanisms. Providing readers with a visual tool, such as a sample action tracker template, can help them monitor these metrics and ensure their meetings lead to tangible results.

Technology serves as a powerful enabler for collecting and analyzing meeting data. Modern platforms such as Zoom, Microsoft Teams, and Slack offer built-in analytics that can capture metrics like attendance, chat engagement, and poll responses. For instance, a virtual meeting organizer can review engagement reports to assess whether participants actively contributed or remained passive. Collaboration tools like Trello, Asana, or Monday.com can further enhance this process by tracking the progress of tasks assigned during meetings. A case study could demonstrate this in action: A hybrid organization used analytics from their virtual platform to identify a drop in engagement during longer sessions, prompting them to shift to shorter, more focused meetings with interactive elements. The result was a significant increase in participation and satisfaction.

Data also plays a pivotal role in fostering a feedback loop for continuous improvement. By tracking metrics over time, organizations can assess the impact of changes to meeting practices and refine their approach accordingly. For example, a team that implements stricter timeboxing for agenda items might initially observe improved time efficiency but notice a slight dip in participation as discussions become more constrained. By analyzing this trend, the team can adjust by allocating more time to critical agenda points or incorporating brief moments for open dialogue. This iterative process ensures that meeting practices remain adaptable, responsive, and aligned with participant needs.

Additionally, data provides a foundation for benchmarking and goal-setting, enabling organizations to define clear standards for meeting performance. Teams can establish targets such as reducing average meeting duration by 20%

or achieving a 90% completion rate for follow-up tasks. These benchmarks not only guide improvement efforts but also create motivation and accountability within the organization. For instance, a department that consistently meets or exceeds its benchmarks for stakeholder satisfaction might use its data-driven approach as a model for other teams. Providing readers with a visual example, such as a graph comparing meeting performance metrics before and after implementing changes, can help illustrate the power of benchmarking and progress tracking.

The role of data in refining meeting processes cannot be overstated. It transforms meetings from subjective experiences into measurable, actionable components of organizational success. By quantifying performance, leveraging technology, fostering feedback loops, and setting benchmarks, data provides the foundation for meaningful and sustainable improvements. Case studies, such as the hybrid organization's use of virtual engagement analytics, demonstrate how data-driven insights can lead to tangible benefits in efficiency and outcomes. Ultimately, integrating data into meeting practices empowers teams to align their efforts with strategic goals, ensuring that every meeting contributes to progress and collaboration.

EMBRACING A DATA-DRIVEN MINDSET

Embracing a data-driven mindset in meetings is a transformative approach that elevates them from routine tasks to strategic opportunities for progress. In many organizations, meetings are judged based on subjective impressions—whether they felt productive or seemed engaging. However, relying solely on perception risks overlooking inefficiencies and missed opportunities for improvement. A data-driven mindset replaces guesswork with evidence, enabling teams to make informed decisions about how to plan, execute, and refine their meetings. By systematically integrating data into meeting practices, organizations can ensure their gatherings are purposeful, results-oriented, and aligned with broader goals.

The foundation of a data-driven mindset lies in understanding the value of information and how it translates into actionable insights. Meetings are complex, involving time, resources, and multiple participants with diverse expectations. Data provides a lens through which these factors can be analyzed objectively. For instance, tracking participation rates can reveal if meetings are inclusive or if certain individuals dominate discussions. Similarly, data on follow-up task completion offers a clear measure of whether decisions made during the meeting translate into actionable outcomes. This shift from subjective assessments to measurable metrics allows teams to identify strengths and address weaknesses, ensuring that meetings consistently deliver value.

Adopting a data-driven approach requires organizations to implement tools and systems that facilitate the collection and analysis of meeting data. Many modern technologies, such as video conferencing platforms and project management software, come equipped with analytics features that make this process seamless. For example, platforms like Zoom or Microsoft Teams can track engagement metrics, such as how long participants stay in the meeting and how often they contribute. Collaboration tools like Trello or Asana can be used to monitor the progress of follow-up tasks. A case study could highlight a company that used engagement analytics from its virtual meeting platform to identify patterns of disengagement during lengthy sessions. By shortening meetings and incorporating interactive elements, they achieved a 25% improvement in participant satisfaction within three months.

However, embracing a data-driven mindset goes beyond collecting numbers; it requires fostering a culture that values and utilizes data. Teams must be encouraged to view data not as a tool for judgment but as a resource for growth. Leadership plays a critical role in modeling this mindset by sharing insights transparently, celebrating improvements, and addressing challenges revealed by data. For instance, if metrics show that meetings frequently run over time, leadership can approach this not as a failure but as an opportunity to explore better agenda management techniques. This approach fosters an environment of trust and collaboration, where participants are motivated to engage with the data-driven process.

One of the most transformative aspects of a data-driven mindset is its capacity to drive innovation in meeting practices. Data often uncovers patterns and insights that may not be immediately apparent through observation alone. For example, if feedback and analytics reveal that discussions in virtual meetings lack depth, teams might experiment with breakout groups or structured brainstorming formats to enhance collaboration. Similarly, data showing a gap in follow-up task completion might inspire the adoption of a task-tracking tool integrated into meeting workflows. These innovations, informed by evidence, help meetings evolve to meet changing needs and ensure they remain relevant and impactful.

Finally, a data-driven mindset aligns meetings with the principles of continuous improvement, ensuring they become more effective over time. By treating each meeting as part of an ongoing feedback loop, teams can refine their processes iteratively. For instance, after implementing a new facilitation method to improve engagement, data can validate whether the change was successful or requires further adjustment. Over time, this cycle of data collection, analysis, and adaptation creates a dynamic process where meetings grow increasingly aligned with their objectives. Including a visual example, such as a graph illustrating improvements in meeting satisfaction or follow-up completion rates over time, can inspire readers to embrace this iterative approach.

A data-driven mindset transforms meetings from subjective experiences into measurable opportunities for organizational growth. By understanding the value of data, leveraging technology, fostering a culture of trust, and using insights to drive innovation, teams can ensure their meetings are purposeful and impactful. Real-world examples, such as the company that improved satisfaction through engagement analytics, demonstrate the tangible benefits of this approach. Ultimately, embracing a data-driven mindset ensures that every meeting is not just an event but a strategic tool for collaboration, decision-making, and progress. In a fast-paced and resource-conscious world, this approach empowers organizations to maximize the value of every interaction.

Chapter 10: Cultivating a Meeting Culture

Meeting culture represents the collective behaviors, attitudes, and practices that an organization adopts regarding how meetings are planned, conducted, and valued. It is more than just the sum of individual meetings—it is the underlying ethos that determines whether meetings drive progress or waste time. A strong meeting culture signals an organization's commitment to collaboration, respect for individuals' contributions, and alignment toward common goals.

At its core, meeting culture influences how people approach their work and interact with one another. Organizations with effective meeting cultures prioritize preparation, purpose, and productivity, ensuring that every meeting adds value. This fosters an environment where teams feel empowered, knowing their time and input are respected. Conversely, when meeting culture is neglected, the result is often disorganized, ineffective gatherings that frustrate participants and erode trust in the process.

Leadership plays a critical role in shaping meeting culture. Leaders set the tone by modeling behaviors that emphasize efficiency, engagement, and inclusivity. When executives and managers demonstrate best practices—such as arriving prepared, staying on topic, and encouraging participation—they signal that meetings are a vital tool for achieving shared success. These actions create a ripple effect, inspiring others to adopt similar behaviors and raising the overall standard of meetings across the organization.

The importance of meeting culture extends beyond individual interactions; it reflects the organization's broader values. Meetings are often a microcosm of the workplace, revealing how teams communicate, make decisions, and collaborate. An organization that prioritizes effective meetings is one that values clarity, accountability, and mutual respect. This alignment not only enhances meeting outcomes but also strengthens the organization's reputation as a place where people can work efficiently and meaningfully.

Cultivating a strong meeting culture requires intention and effort. It begins with a shared understanding of what meetings should accomplish and a commitment to embedding best practices into daily operations. Over time, as these practices become habits, they form the foundation of a culture where meetings consistently drive results and reinforce the organization's mission.

Organizations that invest in their meeting culture reap benefits far beyond improved gatherings. They experience enhanced productivity, better decision-making, and stronger team cohesion. Employees are more engaged and motivated, knowing that their time and ideas are valued. In this way, meeting culture is not just about improving one aspect of the workplace; it is a cornerstone of organizational success.

EMBEDDING BEST PRACTICES IN ORGANIZATIONAL CULTURE

Embedding best practices for meetings into an organization's culture is a transformative step that requires deliberate effort and consistent reinforcement. It is about moving beyond isolated instances of effective meetings to establish a universal standard that guides how meetings are planned, conducted, and evaluated across the organization. When these practices become ingrained, meetings transition from being potential sources of inefficiency to powerful tools for collaboration and progress.

The foundation of embedding best practices lies in setting clear organizational expectations. This starts with developing and communicating standards for meetings that everyone in the organization can follow. These standards might include requiring a clear agenda for every meeting, defining roles such as facilitator and note-taker, and establishing norms for participation, such as active listening and respecting diverse perspectives. By articulating these expectations, organizations provide a framework that ensures consistency and clarity.

Leadership plays a pivotal role in this process. Leaders must exemplify the meeting culture they wish to instill, demonstrating preparation, punctuality, and a commitment to purposeful discussions. When executives and managers model these behaviors, they signal their importance and encourage others to adopt them. This leadership-driven approach ensures that meeting excellence becomes an integral part of the organizational ethos, rather than just a checklist item.

To support the adoption of best practices, organizations can leverage tools and technology that align with their meeting philosophy. Scheduling platforms, shared calendars, and collaboration tools can simplify meeting preparation and follow-up, while video conferencing software and virtual whiteboards enhance engagement for remote or hybrid teams. The key is to integrate these tools seamlessly into workflows, ensuring that they facilitate rather than complicate the process.

Policies and guidelines also play a crucial role in embedding meeting best practices. Organizations can develop standardized templates for agendas and meeting minutes, making it easier for employees to adhere to expectations. Establishing clear criteria for when meetings are necessary—versus when an email or memo might suffice—helps to reduce meeting overload and ensures that time is spent on gatherings that genuinely add value.

Feedback mechanisms are essential to the process of embedding best practices. Regularly soliciting input from employees about their meeting experiences provides valuable insights into what is working and where improvements are needed. Anonymous surveys, team debriefs, or one-on-one conversations can all serve as effective channels for gathering feedback. This iterative approach allows organizations to refine their practices over time, ensuring they remain relevant and effective.

Embedding best practices also requires organizations to acknowledge and address the cultural and operational challenges that may arise. Resistance to change is natural, particularly in environments where poor meeting habits are deeply ingrained. Overcoming this requires consistent communication about the benefits of effective meetings, coupled with a willingness to adapt practices to meet the unique needs of teams and departments.

When best practices are successfully embedded into an organization's culture, they become second nature. Employees approach meetings with a shared understanding of their purpose and an appreciation for the value they can deliver. Teams function more cohesively, decisions are made more efficiently, and the organization as a whole benefits from a renewed focus on collaboration and accountability. Embedding these practices is not just about improving meetings; it is about fostering a culture that supports excellence in every aspect of work.

TRAINING TEAMS FOR CONSISTENT MEETING EXCELLENCE

Training teams for consistent meeting excellence is a critical step in ensuring that best practices are not only understood but also effectively implemented across an organization. While setting clear expectations and embedding guidelines into the culture are essential, training provides the practical tools and confidence individuals need to execute these practices in their daily interactions. It empowers employees at all levels to contribute to meetings that are focused, efficient, and productive.

Effective training begins with identifying the specific needs of the organization and its teams. Different roles require different skills, and tailoring the training to these distinctions ensures relevance and impact. For example, facilitators need to learn how to guide discussions, manage time, and handle conflicts constructively, while participants benefit from understanding how to prepare for meetings, contribute meaningfully, and follow through on action items. By addressing these role-specific requirements, training can create a comprehensive foundation for meeting excellence.

Workshops and interactive sessions are valuable formats for training, as they allow employees to practice skills in a controlled environment. Role-playing scenarios, for instance, can help participants navigate common meeting challenges, such as managing dominant voices, encouraging quiet team members to share their thoughts, or steering conversations back to the agenda. These exercises not only enhance understanding but also build confidence in applying what they've learned to real-world situations.

Training should also focus on equipping employees with the tools and techniques that support effective meetings. This includes instruction on how to create detailed agendas, take accurate meeting notes, and utilize collaboration technologies effectively. In virtual or hybrid environments, additional emphasis may be placed on managing technical tools, maintaining engagement across different formats, and fostering a sense of inclusivity despite physical distances. These practical skills form the backbone of successful meetings.

For training to be impactful, it must go beyond one-time events. Ongoing education and reinforcement are key to sustaining meeting excellence over time. Organizations can achieve this through regular coaching sessions, peer-led discussions, or incorporating meeting-focused modules into broader professional development programs. Providing access to online resources, such as videos, templates, or best-practice guides, ensures employees have continuous opportunities to refine their skills.

Leadership involvement is crucial in driving the success of training initiatives. When leaders participate in and endorse training programs, they demonstrate their commitment to fostering a culture of meeting excellence. This not only reinforces the importance of the initiative but also encourages employees to take it seriously. Managers can further support their teams by providing constructive feedback after meetings, highlighting areas of strength and suggesting improvements where needed.

Organizations can also weave meeting training into their onboarding processes. New employees who learn effective meeting practices as part of their introduction to the company are more likely to adopt these behaviors from the start, contributing to a culture of excellence. This proactive approach ensures that meeting expectations are understood universally, preventing the perpetuation of poor habits.

The benefits of well-trained teams extend far beyond the meeting room. Teams that understand how to collaborate effectively during meetings are better equipped to work together outside of them, leading to improved communication, stronger relationships, and greater overall productivity. Training transforms meetings from an often-dreaded obligation into a tool for achieving shared goals, ultimately strengthening the fabric of the organization itself.

CELEBRATING MEETING SUCCESSES TO REINFORCE HABITS

Celebrating meeting successes is an essential but often overlooked aspect of cultivating a culture of excellence. Recognizing and reinforcing effective meeting behaviors not only solidifies best practices but also motivates teams to maintain high standards. When organizations actively acknowledge successful meetings and the contributions that make them possible, they create a positive feedback loop that encourages consistency and improvement over time.

Success in meetings is defined not just by achieving the desired outcomes but also by how those outcomes are reached. A productive meeting is one where preparation, engagement, collaboration, and follow-through are all evident. Celebrating these achievements starts with identifying what went well and why. Was the agenda followed effectively? Did participants engage in meaningful, respectful discussions? Were decisions made and action items clearly assigned? By spotlighting these elements, organizations can emphasize the behaviors that contribute to successful outcomes.

Recognition can take many forms, ranging from informal acknowledgments to more structured celebrations. A simple thank-you from a manager at the end of a well-run meeting can go a long way in making participants feel valued. Highlighting effective meetings in team updates or organizational newsletters reinforces their importance and provides an opportunity to share lessons learned. For larger successes, such as a meeting that resolved a critical issue or launched a significant initiative, more visible recognition—like awards or shoutouts in company-wide communications—can amplify the impact.

Sharing success stories is another powerful way to celebrate and reinforce good meeting habits. Case studies or testimonials about effective meetings can serve as both recognition and a learning tool for others. For example, detailing how a cross-functional team used a well-facilitated brainstorming session to develop an innovative solution demonstrates the tangible benefits of effective meeting practices. These stories provide inspiration and concrete examples that other teams can emulate.

Feedback plays a central role in celebration and reinforcement. Post-meeting surveys or debriefs can help identify what worked particularly well, giving participants an opportunity to reflect on their contributions and successes. Positive feedback should be shared openly to encourage a sense of pride and achievement, while constructive insights can be framed as opportunities for growth. This balanced approach ensures that teams remain focused on continuous improvement without diminishing their accomplishments.

Encouraging a culture of feedback and recognition requires consistency and intentionality. Leaders must be proactive in acknowledging meeting successes and fostering an environment where these celebrations are normalized. For example, starting meetings with a brief acknowledgment of previous successes or ending them by reflecting on what went well can integrate celebration into the regular rhythm of work. This habit reinforces the idea that every meeting is an opportunity to contribute to the organization's success.

Celebrating meeting successes is also an opportunity to highlight the connection between effective meetings and broader organizational goals. When teams see how their efforts in the meeting room translate into tangible results—such as achieving project milestones, solving customer problems, or driving innovation—they are more likely to embrace and sustain best practices. This alignment between individual actions and organizational outcomes creates a sense of purpose and motivation.

By celebrating successes, organizations not only reinforce good meeting habits but also foster a culture of appreciation and positivity. Teams feel recognized and valued, which strengthens engagement and collaboration. Over time, these celebrations build momentum, turning effective meetings into a hallmark of the organization and a source of pride for employees. This simple yet impactful practice ensures that meeting excellence is not just a goal but a lasting reality.

BUILDING A LEGACY OF EFFECTIVE MEETINGS

Building a legacy of effective meetings means creating a lasting framework where exceptional meeting practices are ingrained in an organization's DNA. It is not about achieving temporary improvements but about ensuring that the principles of well-conducted meetings persist across teams, leaders, and even organizational changes. A legacy of meeting excellence reflects a culture where purposeful, productive discussions are central to collaboration, decision-making, and progress.

A key element of this legacy is consistency. Effective meetings should not be the exception but the standard. To achieve this, organizations must maintain clear expectations and continually reinforce the importance of preparation, engagement, and follow-through. This requires a sustained commitment to best practices, with leaders and teams embracing their roles as stewards of meeting excellence.

Leadership plays a pivotal role in building this legacy. Leaders set the tone for what is acceptable and valued in meetings, and their behaviors serve as a model for others. When leaders prioritize well-structured agendas, meaningful participation, and actionable outcomes, they establish a precedent that encourages others to follow suit. Leadership continuity in upholding these practices ensures that the commitment to effective meetings becomes a permanent feature of the organization.

Institutional memory is another critical factor. Organizations should document their meeting standards and practices, creating resources that can guide future employees and leaders. This includes templates, guidelines, and training materials that encapsulate the principles of effective meetings. By preserving this knowledge, organizations safeguard against the loss of progress when personnel or leadership changes occur.

The legacy of effective meetings also depends on adaptability. As teams, technologies, and business environments evolve, so must meeting practices. Organizations that embrace feedback and continuously refine their approach to meetings ensure that their practices remain relevant and impactful. Regular assessments of meeting effectiveness, informed by participant feedback and organizational outcomes, allow teams to identify areas for improvement and innovate in response to new challenges.

A lasting culture of effective meetings requires embedding these practices into every facet of the organization. From onboarding new hires to training future leaders, the principles of meeting excellence should be woven into the fabric of professional development. When employees are introduced to these expectations early and see them consistently reinforced, they internalize them as an integral part of the organization's values.

Celebration and recognition also play a role in sustaining this legacy. By acknowledging meeting successes and the individuals or teams that exemplify best practices, organizations reinforce their importance and inspire others to contribute to this culture. Over time, these celebrations build pride and ownership in the organization's ability to conduct meetings that matter.

Ultimately, the legacy of effective meetings is reflected in the outcomes they achieve. Organizations with a strong meeting culture consistently drive better decisions, foster stronger collaboration, and achieve their goals more efficiently. This legacy not only benefits the organization but also enhances the professional experience of every individual involved. Meetings are no longer viewed as a drain on time but as valuable opportunities to connect, create, and deliver results.

A legacy of effective meetings is about more than just maintaining standards—it is about inspiring a mindset where excellence is the default. It ensures that the tools and habits established today will continue to empower teams and leaders for years to come, leaving an enduring mark on the organization's success. By committing to this vision, organizations can transform their approach to meetings and secure a future where collaboration and productivity thrive.

Discover more

Author

Other books

www.ingramcontent.com/pod-product-compliance
Lightning Source LLC
Chambersburg PA
CBHW071652240526
45469CB00021B/2189